THE
ELECTRONIC OFFICE

E 70

THE
ELECTRONIC OFFICE

NANCY B. FINN
Boston University

Prentice-Hall, Inc., Englewood Cliffs, New Jersey 07632

Library of Congress Cataloging in Publication Data

Finn, Nancy B.
  The electronic office.

  Bibliography: p.
  Includes index.
    1. Business—Data processing. 2. Electronic data
processing. 3. Office practice—Automation. I. Title.
HF5548.2.F457 1983   651.8'4   82-15007
ISBN 0-13-251819-8

Cover by Ray Lundgren
Manufacturing buyer: Ed O'Dougherty

Printed in the United States of America

10 9 8 7 6 5 4 3 2

ISBN 0-13-251819-8

Prentice-Hall International, Inc., *London*
Prentice-Hall of Australia Pty. Limited, *Sydney*
Editora Prentice-Hall do Brasil, Ltda., *Rio de Janeiro*
Prentice-Hall Canada Inc., *Toronto*
Prentice-Hall of India Private Limited, *New Delhi*
Prentice-Hall of Japan, Inc., *Tokyo*
Prentice-Hall of Southeast Asia Pte. Ltd., *Singapore*
Whitehall Books Limited, *Wellington, New Zealand*

*To my parents who gave me an appreciation
of the great wisdom to be learned from the past...
And to my children, who are the future...*

Contents

Foreword

Computers are impinging on our world with increasing audacity. They are becoming difficult to ignore. Not content to remain buried in the fuel injection systems of our cars, nor safely hidden behind the dials of our washing machines, now they confront us at every turn. They dole out our cash, entertain and educate our kids, and do business with us by phone.

Some of us have welcomed this microprocessor migration. We have embraced these tools and have used them to begin transforming our businesses and our lives. Others are more stand-offish, somewhat skeptical, and maybe a little bit scared.

As computers become more affordable and more approachable in their design, we need to take an objective look at what they can really accomplish—How can they help? Where do they fit in?

It is, perhaps, not surprising that Nancy Finn, a specialist in business communications, became interested in the relationship between computers and the office. That fascination led to this book—a book written by a non-computer person for non-computer people.

Nancy spent a year learning how computers are being used in offices today. She interviewed computer users, consultants and equipment manufacturers. Her goal—to help the small business person understand the technology that has become suddenly affordable.

Selecting a computer system for the office can be a trying experience for anyone. It helps to have someone describe the process, and lay the groundwork.

But remember, the most important element you bring to this process is your understanding of your own business. It is not effective to simply automate the steps that are being performed manually in your office. It is crucial to do some soul-searching about what the underlying mission of your enterprise is, before you introduce technology to further that mission.

Finally, bear in mind that the purpose of a computer is to augment the human intellect, not to replace it.

Patricia B. Seybold

Preface

Fact—Approximately one-third of total office costs involve the preparation, duplication, handling, and storage of paper. U.S. industry has over 265 billion documents in storage. This information industry, which has doubled since 1955, accounts for more than half of the Gross National Product.

Fact—In 1950 it cost $1.50 to produce a letter. In 1980 without office automation, it cost $4.85 to produce a single letter.

Fact—Industrial productivity has climbed almost 90 percent during the past decade while office productivity has inched up only 4 percent. Meanwhile, the cost of computer hardware has dropped significantly, putting computers into the reach of every businessman and professional.

Fact—There were approximately 1,000 computers in America in the early 1950s and no microcomputers, microprocessors, or chips. By 1976 there were over 220,000 computers and three-quarters of a million microcomputers in use. By 1980 Americans were using over 10 million microprocessors.

Fact—The calculating capacity of computers costing $1 million in the 1950s is contained in microelectronic circuits that cost less than $20 in the 1980s.

Fact—The number of computer terminals, now estimated at 5 million, is expected to exceed 11.5 million within four years. (*New York Times,* March 28, 1982).

Fact—Staff expenses are expected to grow from the $31 billion spent in 1981 to more than $34.5 billion by 1983 (*New York Times,* March 28, 1982).

Fact—We are living in a new era—"The Computer Age"—that through an evolutionary process will change the way we perform the most simple tasks and the most complex projects.

The *office of the future* is viewed by some as a paperless office where everything is processed electronically and all messages are stored on electronic files. "Science fiction," some say. "Reality today," say others.

While the likelihood of a *paperless office* is remote, at least in the twentieth century, businesspeople are realizing that computers with their peripheral electronic devices, such as printers and communicators, are no longer a luxury, nor are they a novelty. Office automation is a necessity with its amazing array of sophisticated word processing equipment, communications equipment, and storage media.

During the next decade, every manager's desk will have a video terminal and in every executive's briefcase there will be a "hand held" computer. These computers will have the capacity to "talk" to terminals in various remote locations. Information will be at one's fingertips.

Office automation is an evolutionary process—one that will require patience, understanding and the willingness of the individuals involved in the office to adapt to new ways of doing things.

Marshall McLuhan, in his book *Understanding Media: The Extensions of Man,* wrote the often quoted phrase, "the medium is the message...." Mr. McLuhan contends that a "medium is an extension of ourselves and the message of the medium is the change that it introduces in human affairs...."

The computer is a new medium—one that will bring about great change to the affairs of business. At the core of this change will be new ways to communicate.

Communication has been referred to as the "glue" that holds computer technology together. In the next decade, as information processing takes hold in the office, it is in the processes of communication where office automation will have its greatest impact.

The manipulation of information has always been a key focus of business. Getting a piece of information from point A to point B in a way in which the information is not merely passed along but is understood and utilized is what communication is all about.

Paper and the telephone have traditionally been the common tools of communication in the office. They will gradually give way to electronics which will alter our normal patterns of doing business.

Great challenges are ahead. The computer invites mankind to find new ways to solve problems and to handle programs that have been left untouched in the past for lack of a feasible way to accomplish the task. The new technology, while promising great potential also threatens chaos.

A way must be found to integrate computer equipment into the office, as it is already structured, so that the human beings who work in that office do not view automation as a threat but as a potential aid to getting the job done.

Computer hardware must become cost-effective, expandable, and compatible so that it is able to interface with a variety of systems and accomplish many tasks. The equipment has to be multifunctional to serve a number of needs.

Computer software must be designed so that it will address individual user needs and enable the user to easily relate to the equipment without a lot of training.

This book, which is written for the business manager, the corporate executive, the professional, in every field, will present an overview of computer technology as it impacts on the office. It is designed to introduce the manager/executive to many of the exciting applications of electronic media as they are being developed right now, by unveiling and untangling such concepts as word processing, business graphics, and decision support systems.

In clear, lucid explanation, this book offers suggestions on how to implement office automation tailored to an individual office's needs. It covers every phase of bringing a computer system into the office from how to shop and where to find an appropriate system, to the legal issues involved in negotiating the computer contract. Practical guidelines are suggested for the purchase of hardware and software. The ergonomic characteristics of computer design as it relates to the office environment are covered, as are specific suggestions on how to form a database once the computer system is in place.

With appropriate graphics and illustrations, the book will cover computer technology of yesterday, today, and tomorrow, including such futuristic concepts as the paperless society, and robotics. Electronic mail, teleconferencing and the intricacies of telecommunications networks will be explored in relation to how each will ultimately bear on the information age.

The book will not discuss the merits of one vendor's system over another, nor will it attempt to describe how to operate particular pieces of equipment. What separates this work from the glut of books and articles currently on the market is its comprehensive scope, written in the nontechnical language of the layman, and presented in a style and format that is dynamic, interesting, and easy to read.

The guidelines and applications described are taken from the practical experience of various offices visited by the author and recounted here. These suggestions are offered to help new users adapt to the technology and adopt it for their own use.

A comprehensive appendix at the end of the book includes a glossary of terms common to the electronic industry—terms that have to be understood by anyone dealing with computers. It also includes a list of books, references, and publications with a short appropriate description to help interested persons become familiar with this industry. Most importantly the appendix contains a series of checklists for the business manager/executive or professional who is planning to purchase a computer system.

The information contained in the book is the result of nearly three years of research, including visits to the premises of computer vendors, computer users in both large and small companies, and extensive interviews with market analysts of computer technology. Many individuals and companies assisted in this research and the author wishes to acknowledge those without whose contributions of time and expertise, this book would not have been written.

ACKNOWLEDGMENTS

Vendor Companies: American Telephone & Telegraph Company, Compugraphic Corporation, Computer Corporation of America, Data General, Digital Equipment Corporation, Honeywell Inc., International Business Machines, Nixdorf Computer Corporation, Peabody Office Furniture, Prime Computer, Raytheon Data Systems, Wang Laboratories, and Xerox Corporation.

User Companies: American Cellophane & Plastics Corporation, Brigham & Women's Hospital, Commercial Union Assurance Companies, First National Bank of Boston, John Hancock Life Insurance Company, Pelham Drug Company of Brookline, MA, The Beacon Companies, and The Boston Company.

Independent Consultants: Howard Anderson of Yankee Group, Vincent Guiliano of Arthur D. Little Inc., Chuck Norris of the International Data Corporation, Patty Seybold of Seybold Publications, Professors James Ware and James McKenney of the Harvard Business School, Professor Richard Lott of Bentley College, and Bolt Beranek & Newman Company.

A special thank to those individuals who gave time and expertise to make this project possible includes Howard Anderson, who started me off on this project; Patty Seybold, whose time, advice, and expertise were invaluable; Murray Copp of Digital Equipment Corporation, whose patience and expert advice was most welcome; Robert M. Leavy, partner Fox & Company; and Jeffrey Finn, who prepared the rough sketches for the art work. Also a special thanks to my typist, Gabrielle A. Brousseau, to my husband, Peter and sons, Jeffrey and David for their patience.

PART ONE

INTRODUCTION: THE PROMISE OF ELECTRONICS

...The promise of electronics is the miracle chip with its ever increasing capacity to handle more and more informational units.

...The promise of electronics is increased productivity accomplished by a labor force that is satisfied with its work.

...The promise of electronics is automated information processing at all levels of management in the office, from the routine clerical activities that will be enhanced by word processing capabilities to decision support systems available for the manager/executive. The promise is text processing, data processing, economic forecasting, information access through databases, storage and retrieval. The promise is business graphics enabling the *visual* drafting of many concepts and ideas; the promise is the personal computer and the miniaturization of components to fit into the briefcase of every worker.

...The promise of electronics is a new technology which changes the office and makes it a better place in which to work.

Chapter One

From Miracle Chips to Mag Cards

American clergyman Henry Ward Beecher, during the mid-1900s, wrote of invention: "A tool is but the extension of a man's hand, and a machine is but a complex tool."

Until the invention of the computer, all mankind's inventions were a means to increased physical power. They were an extension of muscle, enabling man to complete chores more quickly, more easily, and more efficiently. That is what the Industrial Revolution was all about—the ability to extend beyond the limited power of manual labor and utilize the "muscle" power of machines which became more complex and more powerful as they were enlarged and refined.

With the invention of the computer, machines no longer were confined to the extension of physical power. For the first time in the history of civilization, the computer would do for man's brain, what all previous machines had done for his muscles.

It was over a century ago that the first computer was designed by an English mathematician named Charles Babbage. The purpose of this machine was to mechanize the calculation of various logarithmic and astronomical tables. As Mr. Babbage refined his ideas, his machine became more sophisticated and better able to handle various types of mathematical computations.

Babbage's Analytical Engine was powered by steam. Similar to today's computers, it worked from a planned program of operating instructions that were stored on punched cards. The machine had memory, a section for entry of data or instructions, and an output section for printing results.

In 1890 the U.S. Census Bureau employed similar tabulating equipment, powered by electricity, to analyze the statistical data collected that year. The equipment was based on the work of Dr. Herman Hollerith of the Bureau, and many similar punchcard machines were developed in subsequent years based on Hollerith's initial devices.

The "age of the computer" really began in 1939 when Dr. Howard Aiken of Harvard University introduced the "Automatic Sequence Controlled Calculator," or Mark I, built by the International Business Machines Corporation (IBM). The machine required a complex of devices linked by hundreds of miles of wires. Its claim to fame was the ability to perform 23 digit addition and subtraction in three-tenths of a second and the multiplication of two 23-digit numbers in about six seconds. Quite a feat at that time.

The first electronic computer, named "ENIAC" (Electronic Number Integrator and Calculator), was completed in 1946 as World War II increased the demand for faster computations. ENIAC and other similar computers filled whole rooms. ENIAC utilized 140,000 watts of electricity and contained 18,000 vacuum tubes that generated and controlled the electrical current, which enabled it to calculate. It was a mammoth machine that took up a great expanse of space and was costly to operate.

It was the discovery of the transistor in 1947 and the subsequent invention of the silicon chip in 1959 that brought about the age of modern computing.

The silicon chip, or "miracle chip," as it has been dubbed, is the size of a tiny fleck—about a quarter of an inch square and quite flat. Its main component is silicon which, next to oxygen, is the most abundant ingredient found on the earth's surface. This "miracle chip" has the calculating power at least as great as that of a main frame computer that would have filled an entire room. It represents a giant leap in the technology that spawned a computer industry worth many billions of dollars and is expected to grow at a rate of twenty percent annually. The potential is unlimited. Even more powerful chips are envisioned in the future. They bring computer power out of the hands of the specialists and into the office, where all levels of workers, from clerks to executives, will be involved.

During the 1960s and early 1970s, although silicon chips were available, most computing power sat in large mainframes, the overseers of which were data processing specialists. These were the years when data processing came to fruition. The large mainframes were accessed by one or

1983	Voice technology begins to appear in systems. Electronic mail takes hold. Decision support and business graphics assumes importance.
1982	The personal computer proliferates on the market. Integration becomes the watchword, and the industry looks to a "Systems" approach.
1981	The "Writers" (small word processing standalones) are established. First executive workstation introduced by Xerox.
1980	Word processing becomes a common term for most corporate offices. Many shared resource systems introduced.
1979	Electronic "intelligent" typewriters, such as those from Olivetti, Exxon, and IBM, become important in the marketplace. Merging of WP and DP into multi-function systems.
1978	"Office of the Future" concept emerges. First intelligent printer, using fiber optics technology, is introduced by Wang. System prices begin to
1977	drop as more small systems come on the market.
1976	IBM is first on the market with a total information processing system
1975	called "System 6." The system includes diskette storage, magnetic card reader, and CRT with ink jet printer.
1974	Mid-1970s video display terminals become predominant in word processing environment.
1973	Vydec introduces CRT; first to use "floppy disk" storage medium. IBM introduces Mag Card II.
1972	Electronic typewriters emerge.
1971	Over a dozen manufacturers enter the market with text editing systems.
1970	Beginning of the word processing evolutionary impact on the office.
1969	Magnetic Card Selectric MC/ST is introduced.
1968	The "Miracle" Silicon Chip begins to appear in smaller pieces of hardware.
1967	Other early systems begin to appear on the market which use magnetic
1966	tape as a storage medium where typed information is coded on magnetic tape.
1965	"Text Processing" term becomes part of popular business vocabulary. The term was coined by Ulrich Steinhilper.
1964	Magnetic Tape Selectric Typewriter (MTST) was brought out by IBM.

FIGURE 1-1 Information Processing Time Line.

several users for a variety of purposes. Most people thought of computers as being "big machines" that sat in a back room and were useful to do such accounting functions as billing, accounts receivable, accounts payable, inventory, and payroll. Those few managers who used the computer depended upon the data processing specialists to see to it that their work got done. Very few managers ever dreamed that some day they would be sitting at a terminal themselves, dealing with input, output, and memory tapes.

Small businesses that needed computer work rented time on mainframes maintained by service bureaus or by other, larger companies. The owners of these businesses only came into contact with the computer when they had to sign the checks for time rentals on computer mainframes.

FIGURE 1-2   Intel 8086 HMOS 16-bit Microprocessor, Designed to Deliver Ten Times the Processing Power of the 8080, Its Predecessor, and Used in Many of the Smaller Systems Currently on the Market. (*Courtesy of Intel Corporation*)

The invention of the "miracle chip" has brought the magic of computing power out of the hands of the specialist and into the hands of everyone. With the development of the chip came the development of microcomputing and microprocessing—small-scale computing power available to everyone.

The cost of computing power has dropped significantly. In 1951 it cost $1.26 for the computer to do 100,000 multiplications. By 1976, it only cost one cent to complete the same calculations. The technology continues to show a steady, real-cost decline of nearly 17 percent annually. As the density of integrated circuits has doubled over the past decade, both the cost per bit and the physical size of semiconductor random access memory has shrunk more than tenfold.

Advances in chip technology were not the only factors that have brought the concept of the computer out of the back room and into the business office. As data processing specialists developed computer software, it became clear to the industry's vendors that if you manipulate and retrieve text representations of a program, then you could manipulate, store, and retrieve a text representation of a text.

Programmers began experimenting with text—storing it in files and using the program-editing facility on their computers to edit nonprogrammed text. They conducted further experiments in formating that text—adjusting and aligning margins, dividing text into pages and paragraphs, and preparing files for printing "hard copy." The end result was that text editing and formating programs were included with software packages being sold for data processing purposes, and word processing found its way into the office.

Initially the applications of word processing were thought of simply as a better way to type, using a keyboard. In 1964 IBM introduced its MT/ST typewriters (Magnetic Tape Selectric Typewriter)—machines with limited electronics and magnetic tape for storage. The "Magnetic" typewriters were sold as machines that would "increase productivity" and work miracles for secretaries who could now store copy on a memory tape for easy recall and the correction of mistakes and errors. Some thought magnetic typewriters would replace secretaries. It generally did not happen that way. Word processing, its users soon realized, became an efficient way to handle the writing, editing, storing, and printing of business documents that grew out of a need for a faster and better way to deal with the information explosion of the 20th century.

Chapter Two

Human Factors in the Office Environment

The office is a human network of individuals—people with individual problems, idiosyncrasies, habits, attitudes, abilities, and needs. The major task of these people is to generate, manipulate, receive, and distribute information. Much of this information is then passed along to the executive suite for decision making and policy formulation.

Offices have not changed much since the introduction of the typewriter in the late 1800s. Although efficient electronic typewriters came into offices to speed paper production, overall information management has remained static. Little thought has been given to the information processes that occur in the office, and this stability has proven to be a hindrance to business productivity.

Several studies confirm that although industrial productivity in the United States rose 85–90 percent during the decade of the 1970s, office worker productivity (white collar productivity) rose only 4 percent. At the same time, office costs have been rising faster than any other segment of the business world.

A close look at the reasons why industrial productivity has leaped ahead of office productivity reveals that industry has engaged in the kind of capital investment, including the implementation of computing power, to warrant the dramatic rise. In the office, however, capital investment has been nonexistent and computing power has been widely ignored.

The U.S. Department of Labor reported in the late 1970s that the average capital investment per manufacturing worker over the decade has been $25,000, whereas capital investment for the office worker has been only $2,000–$4,000.

According to research compiled by the Yankee Group—market analysts in computers and communication—U.S. business spent $800 billion in 1979 on office operations. Of that amount, $600 billion (75 percent) went to direct costs of compensation and benefits of white collar workers. The remaining $200 billion went to indirect costs of internal support, space, and purchased resources. The Yankee Group projects that if these trends continue, direct office costs could reach $1.6 trillion by 1990 in the United States (Yankee Group Report: *Office Automation: The Human Dimension,* July, 1980).

These soaring costs, coupled with decreasing productivity, have made the office ripe for change. Productivity is defined by economists as a measure of how much is produced on average, per hour worked; it relates to

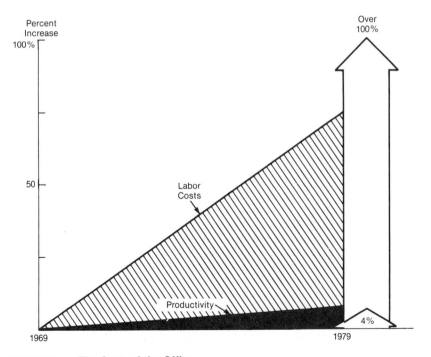

FIGURE 2-1   The State of the Office.
(*Source:* Yankee Group, *Office Automation: The Human Dimension,* July, 1980)

the output of goods and services and to the number of hours of labor it takes to produce those goods and services. In other words, productivity is defined in quantifiable terms.

In the office environment it is difficult to measure the productivity of workers who are primarily engaged in service and information jobs. How do you measure the productivity impact of a decision by an executive who is planning the reorganization of a department? Certainly not in the same way that you measure the unit production of a factory worker.

The need for a major overhaul of office operations has been apparent for some time. It is clear that word processing will play a major role.

According to a study by Booz, Allen and Hamilton, management consultants:

> Managers and professionals spend an average of 25 percent of their time in less productive activities and office automation in the next few years will change that.

The study reports that information retrieval, word processing, and electronic mail will account for "65 percent of the total time-saving potential through 1985."

Automation will eliminate some tasks that are a large part of a paper-based society. Highly routine clerical activities, such as filing and retrieving of information; keying of repetitive documents, or sections of documents; and revisions of reports that are produced with regularity, are obvious chores that can be automated.

Productivity in the office is a double-edged sword. There is the clerical/ secretarial productivity that is fairly easy to quantify in terms of the number of pages manually typed or filed within a certain time span, compared with those same pages typed and filed by a word processor. There is also managerial productivity, which involves a compendium of tasks. Management activity that can be automated includes the following:

1. The preparation of a budget, including the retrieval of past information, current statistics obtained from a data bank; the manipulation of numbers and text on the terminal; the use of graphics to sketch various comparative charts and statistics; the text input and editing of the final budget report, including the drafts and revisions.
2. The generation and reception of mail/messages via an electronic mail system and the elimination of both paper mail and "telephone tag" in the process. Electronic mail systems also enable a manager to work at home, or "telecommute," and to poll employees for suggestions, complaints, input on new proposals, etc.
3. Management travel can be automated with the increasing installation of teleconferencing centers. These facilities would enable the manager to conduct meetings and to reach employees, both inside and outside the company,

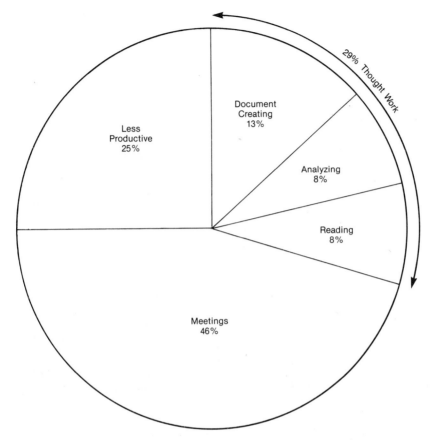

FIGURE 2-2 How Knowledge Workers Spend Their Time—By Activity.
(*Source:* Yankee Group, *Office Automation: The Human Dimension,*
July, 1980)

without the frustration and delays of cancelled flights, traffic jams, and bad
weather.

4. Preparation of reports and proposals.
5. Personal calendar and tickler files to combat some of the tedious daily routines.

Other less obvious responsibilities of managers, such as complex decision
making, budget preparation, and routine administrative functions that currently bog down managers, will also be expedited with the advent of automation.

Studies show that managers work at a fast pace—their activities are
characterized by short, swift tasks and meetings that are not necessarily

continuous. Studies also show that people in an office need a certain amount of privacy; they need to move around; they need positive feedback and recognition. The attitude toward office automation expressed by many office workers is a mixture of:

1. Fear of the unknown.
2. Fear of change.
3. Feelings of ineptness and sometimes inadequacy on the part of managers, who do not wish to be forced to use machinery that they consider alien to them.
4. Fear that computers will displace individuals in the office, including the possible eradication of their own jobs.
5. A genuine annoyance on the part of some who feel that the chore of looking into automation and the implementation of a computer system is merely another burden in their already overcrowded day.

Furthermore, managers and executives fear that a computer will result in employee unrest, lowered morale, disruption of operations, and unjustifiable expense. In some instances, this is just what has happened, when implementation of automation has not been handled with care.

To further complicate matters, middle managers are caught in a squeeze. They must produce results in spite of whatever else is happening in an office. With the introduction of automation, there are slow periods of adjustment from the time the machinery is delivered until the time it is "up and working." "Working" means that all the material important to office functions is input into the computer. This presumes that the people in the office who are going to use the computer have been trained in how to use it. This assumes that the machinery will function without snags, interruptions, and mechanical failures.

As a result, middle managers, who are often the ones in charge of office operations, including the implementation of automation, are not always terribly supportive of the automation process. They resent the normal interruptions of work flow that occur with any change in the pattern and which are compounded by the complexities of automation.

Introducing automation also brings about negative reactions from the service staffers, who are certain that sooner or later they will lose their jobs to the computer. They fear that their skills will become obsolete and that their opportunity for upward mobility no longer exists. They also tend to feel that they are constantly being watched and evaluated by the computer. Instead of regarding it as a tool to help them, they regard the computer as an unfriendly watchdog, monitoring the rate of their production and the number of errors they commit.

It has become quite clear from the experiences of those pioneers of industry, who were the first to try office automation, that there is no simple and clear solution to elevating productivity levels. Although no one will dispute the fact that computers, applied to many office tasks, will increase the speed and efficiency with which these tasks are accomplished, the "quick fix" solution of purchasing expensive electronic equipment, and demanding that office workers learn to use it, will not, by itself, increase productivity. Technology, although playing an important role in productivity improvement, cannot bypass people and the way they react to the performance of their assigned work.

Chapter Three

Automated Information Processing

Automated information processing will be a part of the office in spite of the human elements that would want to push it away. It will take the form of word processing systems; data processing systems that have word processing capability; business graphics systems; and decision support systems.

Experts estimate that since the 1950s, mankind has doubled the amount of new information that has accumulated. And for business, 85 percent of that information is communicated via the written word. Computers provide a better, faster, more efficient way to do business, and in business, that is the name of the game. A new breed of intelligent, microprocessor-based computer terminals are available that can be programmed with software to perform a multitude of functions to assist in information management in the office.

WORD PROCESSING

Word processing is an attempt to do for words what data processing has been doing for numbers—to do away with repetition, boredom, and frustration of doing a job manually when it can be done better and faster by the computer.

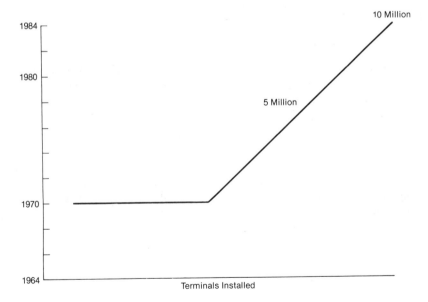

FIGURE 3-1   The Migration to the Electronic Office Begins and Ends with the Terminal.

The Yankee Group conducted studies on document productivity in offices, comparing manual with word processing techniques. The results show that document creation can be quickened 30–50 percent because: "an operator can input on a word processor at rough-draft pace, and such manual activities as erasure and cut and paste are eliminated."

Yankee Group research indicates that "editing on a word processor screen has also proven to be 50–75 percent faster than editing on paper, and that formating and other document preparation tasks require up to 90 percent fewer keystrokes." (Yankee Group, The Technical Office: Analysis and Research, August, 1979). Several research papers have reported that a secretary's productivity can be increased an overall 20–25 percent with a word processor, depending upon how much typing she does.

Bringing word processing to the office, however, is not as simple a task as it might appear. Terminals, which cost between $6,000 and $20,000, are hard to justify as one-to-one replacements for typewriters, which cost between $850 and $1,200. When the concept of word processing was first introduced, vendors tried to cost-justify their products by suggesting that word processing "centers" be formed to replace both existing typing pools and secretarial services, which had generally been handled on a one-to-one basis.

Clustering people to work as word processing technicians failed to address the fact that for office automation to succeed, a basic understanding of the office environment is necessary. Secretarial duties are far broader than just typing. Those who were reshuffled to word processing centers were not available to do the thousand other chores that must be handled by a secretary, such as answering the telephone, coordinating administrative assignments, and engaging in personal relationships with both the boss and clients. The centers were not "tuned in" to the particular idiosyncrasies or needs of a particular manager or department.

Only in situations where centralized word processing replaced centralized typing pools has the concept worked well, because word processing has proven to be a faster means of document production than typing.

Some of the early attempts to implement word processing also failed because the computers were connected from the word processor to a large mainframe. This involved the use of bulky software packages attached to machines that were used to dealing in numbers and not in words. The result was both machine and people confusion and a reduction, rather than an increase, in productivity.

The modern word processing system should perform three major functions: (1) fast document production—especially the production of repetitive documents that can be stored and retrieved; (2) fast and flexible document revision, using such text editing features as insert, delete, and move copy, which are available in every word processing unit; (3) keyboarding of finished quality documents at high speeds. Sophisticated machinery available today also has the capability to perform such information processing applications as search and replace, graphics, repagination, spelling, verification, mathematical computations, sort, and forms completion.

The most basic usage of the word processor is for the secretary to type a document on the keyboard and see it displayed on the screen. She can correct spelling mistakes, change wording, and reorganize paragraphs. The machine then prints out the finished document.

There is little savings in using a word processor rather than a fast electric typewriter to type a single letter. However, when that letter has to be used several times with, perhaps, minor changes, the secretary has only to type the letter once and make the changes in a fraction of the time it would have taken to retype the letter again.

The Word Processing Impact on Letters, Memos, Reports, and Proposals

What word processing will not do is change the need for clear, concise business communication. The technology is only a means to an end—the communicating of important messages among individuals. Word processing will only assist in preventing the current communication clutter by offering better, faster media on which to generate and store messages. The need for correct grammar and spelling does not wash away with the use of computers.

Although many newer computer models have built-in dictionaries to check and verify spelling, the meaning and clarity of a message will only be altered by an individual, not by a computer.

Clear, crisp writing—that avoids long complex explanations when simple ones will do; writing that avoids the use of long words when simple one-syllable words are better; writing that uses concrete terms, not abstractions that need detailed definitions to make them understandable—is still an essential part of better business communication, whether it is to be conveyed by paper or by a computer.

What word processing does do to change business communications' effectiveness is to enable people to manipulate words and paragraphs without having to rekeyboard. As a result, managers are able to make changes in text copy as often as necessary, without undue pressure or loss of time.

The purpose of a business letter or memorandum is to communicate a short message from one party to another. Generally, a letter is used when the communication needs to be sent outside the organization, and a memo is used when the communication is sent within an organization.

FIGURE 3-2   Wangwriter: The High-Performance Word Processor At An Affordable
Price. The Wangwriter's powerful word processing makes it easy to
type letters, memos, and reports faster, with no errors. The
Wangwriter can also perform a variety of personal computing applications, using the CP/M^R operating system. In addition, telecommunications options allow the Wangwriter to link to other Wang systems, as
well as to a variety of other business equipment. Pricing for the workstation, keyboard, printer console and software begins at $6,400 U.S.
(Courtesy of Wang Laboratories)

Word processing terminals enable an office to store key phrases, sentences, and paragraphs of letters or memos. Successful business letters and
memos are well organized. The computer's manipulation powers enable the
writer of business communications to outline ideas; change words and
phrases; bring sentences from one page to another; and correct the grammatical and spelling errors that so frequently appear in today's business
communications. The computer's sort, merge, and search capabilities
enable the writer of business communications to maintain a list of saluta-
tions, names, and addresses of those people with whom he/she frequently

FIGURE 3-3 The Aries I/Aquarius I Secretarial Workstation, Complete with a 70-page Diskette Drive and Word Processing Software. In addition to providing word processing capabilities, the Aquarius I/Aries I secretarial workstation offers several unique features designed to make working with office automation easier and less complicated. WINDOWING, for example, enables secretaries to divide the CRT screen into separate areas so that several documents can be viewed simultaneously. FASTPATH accommodates office interruptions by allowing secretaries to jump quickly from one task to another, then return to the exact place where the interruption took place. (*Courtesy of Syntrex Inc.*)

corresponds and to merge those into a new document that he/she has created, without having to remember the "right" salutation or "correct name spelling."

This is called list processing, or the capability to place a master list on a permanent memory file and call up this list whenever it is needed for incorporation into a general mailing or a specific document.

Word processors are also able to store forms that many businesses find it necessary to use over and over again. These forms can be brought up on the screen and the blanks are filled in by an operator who does not have to spend his/her time adjusting the paper, aligning the document, and typing in the answers.

Business Reports

The Business Report is a written communication that transmits detailed information to a specialized audience. Generally the business report involves research, investigation, and the merging of text matter and data. It is usually a lengthy document. Many business reports include bibliographies and glossaries, which define terminology and documentation. Many business reports are also updated frequently or are issued annually.

Word processing technology has had a marked impact upon the preparation and dissemination of the business report. The ability of word processors to access information from large data bases; from computer banks and from mainframes, enables the writer of a business report to procure and present a more accurate and detailed picture of a situation. The ability of computers to communicate with one another enables the writer of a report to have the data and graphics at his/her fingertips. For example, a statistical chart showing budget projections, which is stored in a data processor, can be accessed by a word processor at another location via a telephone link. It can be imprinted right into the body of a report without ever having to be rekeyboarded. As more and more databases become available, finding the material for business reports will become easier.

Completed reports can be stored on disks with bibliography, glossary, documentation, and other key paragraphs and sentences available for retrieval and insertion into other reports. Statistical data that is already stored has only to be updated, saving time and effort.

Proposals

The business proposal is a written piece designed to request funding or support for a particular project or an idea. Its purpose is to present in clear, lucid, and persuasive terms why the idea in the proposal warrants the expenditure of time, effort, and money. All proposal documents have one objective— to sell! They must be persuasive. All proposals must include extensively outlined budget documentation to support their thesis. It is evident from the capabilities of word processing that, as is the case with the business report, the proposal can be researched and written with far greater ease. The ability to manipulate data; to change paragraphs and sentences; to move blocks of copy from one section of the document to another; to access databases for the documentation of the proposal; to retain on a file various forms that could be used in the budget section of the proposal—all lend themselves to the use of word processing to provide more thorough quality documents. The computation required in budget preparation for a proposal will also be greatly facilitated by the computer's remarkable ability to do these computations with far more speed and more ease than any human.

Phototypesetting

For many offices, the input and manipulation of text on a computer does not fulfill their entire need. A vital step—the need to set that text in

FIGURE 3-4 Itek Phototypesetter.

type—is missing. Technology has provided an answer in the form of the interfacing of word processors to direct-input typesetters. The key here is to set in type the text created on a word processor without having to rekeyboard. In the early days of word processing, this feat was accomplished through the use of "black boxes," which were bulky and expensive. These "black boxes" were attached on each end and provided the interface mechanism to communicate between word processors and teletypewriters. Now an interface can be accomplished using mere telephone lines with the proper communications protocols attached to the machines at each end; or through a cable if the phototypesetter is a matter of a few feet away from the word processing workstation.

Research has clearly indicated that typeset material is easier to read, increases comprehension and retention, reduces the bulk of text, is more attractive and, ultimately, costs less to reproduce. New machinery available not only avoids the double rekeyboarding syndrome, but also avoids having to reproof copy and run corrections.

Phototypesetters take material from almost any communicating word processor. Most phototypesetters are capable of taking material from up to five different input devices, such as word processors, data processors, graphics terminals, optical character readers, and facsimile machines.

In such fields as engineering, law, insurance, marketing and education,

FIGURE 3-5 Compugraphic Phototypesetter.

huge volumes of information are being published and a word processing/phototypesetting interface is a practical advantage. In fields such as public relations, graphic arts, and publishing, which have always used phototypesetting, new technology makes possible the automatic transmission of copy to the typesetting equipment with great savings of time and expense.

Office photocomposers range in price and sophistication from the smaller standalone or direct-entry units to large integrated typesetting systems. The most sophisticated systems include complete page makeup capabilities and can even digitize photographs. These machines run into the hundreds of thousands of dollars and are limited in their use to large newspaper and publishing applications.

Ideally, the ultimate would be to input text at the word processor by the originator of a document and automatically send the text to a photocompositor machine that automatically places it on a page and sends it on to a printer for final reproduction. The incorporation of all these steps at a reasonable cost is in the future. The potential is there, however, and its resultant impact upon paper reduction and the elimination of repetitive manual steps is enormous.

DATA PROCESSING

Data processing, or the processing of "facts and figures" essential to the "running" of an office is also a part of the overall office automation scheme. In many companies the implementation of office automation springs not from the introduction of word processing technology to an otherwise unsophisticated, unknowing management, but from the already existing data processing technology which has been a part of the business for many years.

As farsighted data processing specialists have perceived office needs of the 1980s and beyond, bringing the computer out of the back room has become a way to expand computer power in the company and relieve the office of the growing paperwork burden that many companies experience as their data processing needs expand.

Originally, the use of computers in business was encouraged as the way to get the greatest possible amount of information processed in the shortest time and at the lowest cost. Data processing, in combination with office automation, however, also concerns itself with how well it furthers the mission of the business and how the data processing function improves the productivity of all the office workers.

In larger corporations, data processing is done on several levels: There are the huge mainframe computers, such as the IBM 370 or the Sperry Univac 1100 series, that large companies and financial institutions must have to maintain a semblance of order in their transactions. There are also the minicomputers, such as the DEC PDP 11 or the Data General M/6000, handling smaller, less complex transactions. Many companies slowly have real-

FIGURE 3-6   Nixdorf Data Processor.

FIGURE 3-7 IBM System 34.

ized that although the larger mainframes and minicomputers are necessary to the business, it is also necessary to bring computer power to the desks of many workers via smaller minicomputers and small business computers, placed at strategic locations, which can communicate with each other and with a host. Thus, grew the concept of distributed data processing, which has been a giant step in the direction of office automation.

The impact of all this has been a rather confused approach to office automation and, in many instances, a power struggle between the individual departments and the data processing specialists. The situation has been further complicated by the fact that in most large companies, data processing is viewed as a company-wide concern and office automation as more of a support function for specific tasks.

Put quite simply, however, the data processing structure in control cannot compete with the flexibility of smaller computers and must give way to allow these terminals to proliferate. Many end users, especially those in large companies, are fed up with the long delays they experience in getting new applications or waiting for reports or analyses from an overburdened data processing group. Individualized computing power will satisfy the particular needs of departments and individuals while complimenting the powerful accomplishments of data processing departments. As the multifunctionality of terminals continues to grow, businesses will find that office automation and data processing are inextricably linked to the general welfare of the organization as a whole.

BUSINESS GRAPHICS

Computer graphics is simply the ability of a computer to present data in the form of pictures, rather than in textual or statistical formats. These pictures are designed to help managers and executives better understand the trends and relationships in that data. Improved quality and reduced costs are making computer graphics increasingly feasible in the office automation scheme.

Most astute businessmen have realized for a long time the value of graphs and charts to help them in planning, making decisions, and making presentations. Generally, those visuals have been done by a graphics art department and in some cases by an employee with minimal drawing skills.

Computer graphics have opened up new and exciting possibilities for accomplishing visual communication in business planning and presenta-

FIGURE 3-8   **Wang 2200 Systems. Every Wang 2200 computer system is offered with a wide choice of workstations, which feature superb human engineering; an easy-to-read 12-inch diagonal screen with dual-intensity blinking characters and an underlining capability; business graphics for display of bar graphs and charts; and a familiar typewriter-like keyboard with a ten-key numeric pad for fast data entry. The key features of the Wang 2236DE terminal, for example, are character and line graphics, reverse video, dual intensity and the ability to print screens. The terminal also has a high quality display screen, which is designed to ease the burden of intensive data entry.**
(Courtesy of Wang Laboratories)

tions. The plummeting costs of the hardware needed to provide computer graphics versus the rising cost of labor to produce manual graphics, and the introduction of software that responds to English language commands, are contributing factors in bringing this technology to the office.

As the cost of computer graphics continues to drop and better graphics capabilities are offered by some of the low-cost standalone computers, these computers will become a common medium for an executive to communicate with his employees and clients, and for middle management to communicate the results of their progress *up* to top management. All kinds of data will be filtering both up and down an organization.

The specific purposes of business graphics are to:

1. Make information more visible to managers who are limited in the time they have to review these printouts.
2. Develop charts from the data already in the computer at a lower cost than when they are produced manually.
3. Create charts from data that are not already in the computer.
4. Improve the quality of graphic presentations.
5. Increase the rate at which the data can be absorbed by the manager/executive so that better decision making will take place.
6. Reduce errors that might occur during manual plotting or typing of data.

As a compliment to executive information systems, computer graphics will be one of the single most important contributions to productivity. In decision support, 90 percent of the effort is involved in data gathering and only 10 percent in actual analysis. With computer graphics, much of the legwork of data gathering will be eliminated.

FIGURE 3-9   Data General Graphics Terminal.

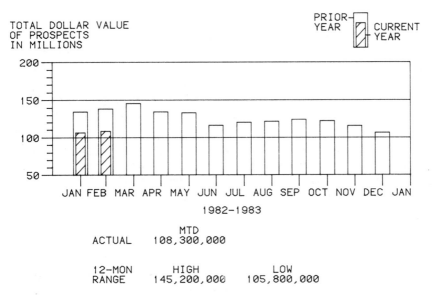

NEW BUSINESS PROSPECTS
SUMMARY - FEBRUARY 1982

TOTAL DOLLAR VALUE
OF PROSPECTS
IN MILLIONS

PRIOR-YEAR   CURRENT YEAR

1982-1983

	MTD
ACTUAL	108,300,000

12-MON RANGE	HIGH 145,200,000	LOW 105,800,000

FIGURE 3-10   A Computer Graphics Printout for Business Analysis.

With systems coming on the market in the early 1980s that utilize a light pen instead of the standard keyboarding required in other computer technologies, executive resistance will be easily overcome.

The applications of business graphics offer several promising and exciting new horizons. Performance monitoring or using the data already in the computer to graphically illustrate such things as financial marketing, operations, and project control is a natural and obvious use of business graphics. By having these illustrations in the computer, there is a continuous facility for easily updating material as information changes. For example, an executive can obtain an up to the minute comparison of company expenditures on a daily, weekly, or monthly basis, depending upon the immediate need. The use of computer graphics in marketing or using these visuals to convince a client that the product or service that you are selling is sound, economically and structurally, is another important feature of graphics application. Computer graphics also have had broad applications in technical presentations when visuals are essential to the understanding of highly detailed or scientific information. These graphics will become more common in presentations as the use of teleconferencing centers increases.

Almost all companies can use computer graphics. Not as many can afford it. Although the costs are rapidly decreasing, there is still a wide margin between what is cost justifiable and what is desirable. To account for some of this overlap, there are time sharing services which for a nominal fee enable a user to make an investment in hardware and will provide the software and the finished product for a set fee.

Many graphics applications can also be run on some of the $70,000–$100,000 minicomputers, or with appropriate software on mainframes, that already exist in companies.

Computer graphics is one of the fastest growing segments of the industry. It will increase in use for both serious statistical data as well as a way for management to convey a message to the employees, with a new and different twist, that is only possible with a visual.

With the increasing linkings between the generation of graphics on the computer and its output in the form of paper, slides, and perhaps, in the future, in other audiovisual media, computer graphics certainly enhances business communication and adds credence to the promise of electronics.

DECISION SUPPORT SYSTEMS

The concept of decision support has taken hold in the 1980s as a part of the office automation scheme. The Yankee Group described it aptly in September of 1980, in their report on Small Business Computing Systems, when

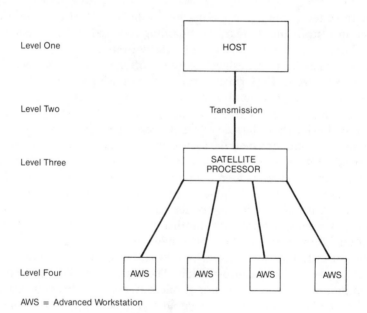

AWS = Advanced Workstation

FIGURE 3-11   Four-Tier Processing.
(*Source:* The Yankee Group)

they talked of a four-tier processing plan that includes the host at level one; transmission at level two; the satellite processors at level three; and the "advanced workstation" at level four (see diagram).

The advanced workstation, the Yankee Group says, is a "low cost" $2,000–$3,500 desktop computer that is software driven, modular, with excellent communications capabilities and is able to run computer programs independent of any high-level computer facility. One of the features of the advanced workstation is its ability to utilize available software packages that will be shared and held in libraries. Each advanced workstation user can access the library files requesting any application in the library.

Applications of decision support systems that are tailored for the manager/executive of the business will include: providing a calendar and a tickler file; document analysis; financial planning; economic forecasting; budget analysis; modeling; accessing databases; and serving as an electronic mailbox. The terminal will also be capable of performing such ordinary functions of a word processor as text editing and of a data processor as basic calculations and data manipulation. Some of the more advanced terminals will have graphics capabilities that will range from the simple bar graphs and pie charts to complex graphics.

With communications, these terminals will handle conference scheduling, and telephone call placements. They will help the manager avoid such snags as missed appointments, doubled up meetings, missed action due dates, and "telephone tag." They will assist managers in preparing their budgets and in keeping track of employee performance in such areas as sales volume, inventory control, etc. In some cases decision support systems will even result in the elimination of extra travel, as they are tied into teleconferencing centers, which will proliferate in offices during the next decade.

PERSONAL COMPUTERS AS EXECUTIVE WORKSTATIONS

Personal computers came on the market as an outgrowth of the small home computer designed for games and simple calculations. The uniqueness of personal computers is that these systems can be plugged into any wall outlet and begin working immediately. Most brands of personal computer use a Z–80 based microprocessor developed by Zilog Inc. of Cupertino, California. They are standalones and they do not have to be professionally programmed before they are used. Many of the systems introduced during the early 1980s utilize an operating system, C.P.M. (Control Program for Microprocessors) developed by Digital Research Inc. of Pacific Grove, California. This operating system works with the Z–80 microprocessors,

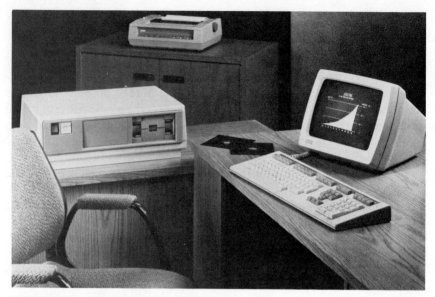

FIGURE 3-12   DEC Personal Computer.

and the combination enables the end user to choose from literally hundreds of application programs that are compatible with their computer and are easy to use (user friendly).

Every personal computer consists of essentially the same components; a microprocessor that executes the instructions given to it by the end user; between 32,000 and 64,000 bytes of memory (a byte is roughly equivalent to one character of working memory); a video display and either a matrix (high speed) or letter quality printer.

There were 200,000 desktop computers shipped in the U.S. during 1979 and the number is expected to grow to 849,000 by 1984 (International Data Corporation estimate). Because there are 2.5 million self-employed professionals in the United States and 15 million managers employed in larger companies, the potential for the personal computer's impact in the office environment as decision support terminals is enormous. Furthermore, because the cost of a personal computer is low—hovering between $3,000 and $5,000— they do not usually require executive level approval or purchase. Instead, they can be buried in departmental budgets as "office equipment" or "spare parts." Their ease of use enables managers to sit down and become proficient in their use within a matter of hours—another reason why they will proliferate in the executive suite. Some executives have even paid for them out of their own pockets, because they have become not only an adjunct to satisfactory task completion but a status symbol as well.

Professionals and managers who have been using personal computers apply them to tasks that are as varied as are their own jobs and personalities. With the graphics that can be found on such systems as the IBM and the Apple computers, they accomplish not only data manipulation, but design work as well. Research has shown that when a professional or manager's job is quantifiable, a decision support terminal can be cost justified. For example, an engineering department that, "unautomated," turns out 500 pages of specifications monthly, and automated turns out 680 pages, can show that the decision support system is necessary. These systems also assist in situations when speed is essential in the communication of information.

The development of *VisiCalc,* an application program that helps the user construct and analyze revenue and expense forecasts, has been a revolutionary impetus to the proliferation of personal computers in the office. VisiCalc is user oriented and user friendly. It has changed the way in which the writers of software programs are approaching their task, and provides many practical, useful, and simple programs. Today, every personal computer is able to use some form of a VisiCalc program or the CP/M "super-

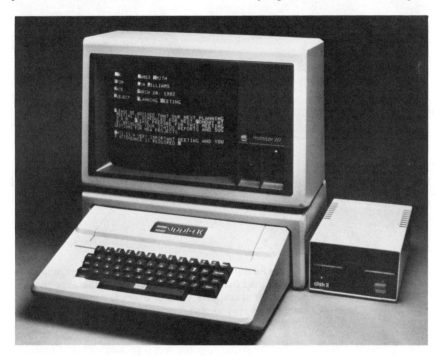

FIGURE 3-13   The Apple II Plus Personal Computer System. This system, equipped with a Monitor *III,* a Disk II floppy disk drive, and Apple Writer software, provides a powerful text editing capability that enables users to write, revise, edit, and print a wide range of documents quickly and easily.
(*Courtesy of Apple Computer, Inc.*)

FIGURE 3–14 **The Apple II Plus Personal Computer System. This system, equipped with a Monitor *III*, two Disk II floppy disk drives, a Silentype thermal printer, and Apple Plot software, enables users to convert any numerical information into easy-to-read charts and graphs.**
(Courtesy of Apple Computer, Inc.)

calc'' program. Easier software programs for word processing applications have also resulted in allaying the fears of managers and executives who were intimidated by the machines.

The Xerox Star

Along with the low priced personal computers that can serve as decision support systems, there is a place for a higher priced workstation for the professional or "knowledge worker," and the Xerox Corporation was the first to introduce this concept in the form of the Xerox Star. The Star incorporates all the necessary ingredients for a professional workstation—namely a terminal that is rich in function, simple and consistent to operate, and is reasonably affordable—with an introductory price tag of $16,595, not including the printer. The Star contains a screen with a display area of 10.4 × 13,12—large enough to accommodate an 8½ × 11 page display plus a display of command information located in the right corner. The keyboard is identical to that of a standard typewriter and a "mouse" with dual control serves as a cursor which moves around the display and works on materials presented on the screen.

The Star includes graphics ability with two distinct types of graphics: (1) charts that present data in pictorial form, such as bar charts, line graphs, and pie charts and (2) simple line drawings. Both capabilities are remark-

FIGURE 3–15   Xerox Star. Wide range of text and graphic information can be created on two-page display screen of newly announced Xerox 8010 Star information system. Designed for use by business professionals, Star system offers a variety of type faces and sizes to choose from, as well as graphics capabilities that will allow users to create their own business illustrations. Most Star functions are available to user by selection—simply by moving a pointer and pressing a key.
(Courtesy Xerox Corporation)

ably easy to use and very effective. By entering the data in the Star, the terminal will draw charts and graphs for you. You can change the graph by changing the style, or parameters you have specified by editing the input data. You can also add information to finished graphs, using normal system editing conventions. You can draw your own diagrams on the Star. The computer will provide you with transfer sheets and all the tools you need. The Star has software that will automatically adjust the size of tabular columns as the user enters data in those columns so he does not have to worry about how wide the various columns should be. Other facilities include the ability to move copy, delete, and insert materials. The system contains a spelling check capability and can be programmed by the user through a built-in user programming language called CUSP (customer programming) that enables the user to write his own applications using English commands.

The Star can operate as a standalone unit or as part of a larger network scheme. It is the first of many terminals designed for a worker who considers himself worthy of a higher priced machine that has a lot more to offer than a desk-top computer.

Decision support systems that contain business graphics, data processing, and word processing technologies are a large part of the office scheme of tomorrow. Each of these technologies taken individually as well as workstations that incorporate all, will provide the automated information processing needed in the coming years.

APPLICATIONS

Information processing applications have found their way into every conceivable business and profession. In law offices, insurance companies, medical offices, accounting firms, small businesses, and manufacturing concerns, the uses of word processing are as varied as are the users.

Many of the newer units have built-in dictionaries with the ability to check for misspelling in seconds. This should be an aid to the manager who has never really learned the proper grammatical or spelling skills in spite of all his years of college and graduate school.

Law

There is no profession that generates as much verbiage on a daily basis as the legal profession. Law offices, therefore, are a natural outlet for office automation technology and have been among the first group to broadly adopt word processing and small business computers.

Law firms that engage in a heavy litigation practice, for example, generate a number of repetitive documents, which are the clearest evidence of the need for word processing. Many firms, recognizing that these repetitive documents have needed some uniformity and condensation have utilized forms in the past.

These forms can all be put into a computer with merely the blanks left to be filled in, saving many hours of a secretary's time each day.

Interrogatories, where questions are standard and only the answers need to be changed, can be stored on a computer disk, as can such documents as medical affadavits, and much of the correspondence of a busy law office.

The indexing and storage features of word processors allow law offices to categorize and catalogue their files. For example, a law firm's memoranda of law files can be copied from the original documents and the text stored by the word processor, thus creating a separate file. An index may then be developed to categorize these memoranda of law files by topic and subject for future cross referencing.

Other applications of word processing include a stored "library" of commonly used paragraphs and phrases, contracts, and wills, which can be constructed "piecemeal," using the original documents and adding in the new variables. These documents can be passed along to the attorneys for corrections and additions, which are inserted without retyping the entire piece. The time savings multiply with each draft. It is not uncommon for a legal document to undergo 15 or 20 revisions before it is finalized.

Many word processors are equipped with automatic revision markers to facilitate the process of proofreading legal documents. Because they must be error-free, this capability is important.

Legal research too, takes a chunk of a lawyer's time. Databases, such as *Lexis, Juris,* and *West Law,* are available to provide attorneys with an almost instantaneous answer to a search for nearly every case recorded in jurisprudence.

Law firms also have some basic data processing needs that a business computer greatly facilitates. Records management, including an inventory of the various attorneys in the office for appropriate billing, is essential to a busy law office. Although a simple fee for services rendered may be suitable for many cases, there are also special arrangements between clients and attorneys for cases which involve a retainer or are billed at different rates for hours and out-of-pocket expenses. A business computer with its appropriate software is able to track these more complicated billing arrangements, saving hundreds of hours and thousands of dollars.

Law firms also have the usual accounts payables for the obvious expenses of the office including rent, electric, supplies, the service of outside consultants, etc. Like every other business, law firms have payroll to meet each week and a general ledger to keep. Even the smallest law office today can afford a small computer to better manage its affairs.

Banking

Banking is another industry where automated applications have revolutionized the way that communications are processed. The potential for the future is even more exciting. Because the primary function of a bank is the transfer and storage of money, every transaction must be supported by exact documentation. Constantly updated information must be available to the bank's customers and officers about accounts and ongoing transactions. Two types of documents dominate a bank's word processing output. The one-page customer communication, such as a letter or postcard. These are typed from a stored original, with variables added in. The second category includes the various statistical reports, usually issued monthly.

Most banks started out by using word processing in central pools. Once they saw how easily the system worked, many individual departments adopted terminals for a variety of uses, from the design of graphics materials to the production of reports that require yearly updates.

One large Boston area bank now produces, on a word processor, an internal telephone directory that used to take months to update. Now, each department keeps its own listing on a disk and merely inserts and deletes names and telephone numbers as they occur. All the disks are merged once a year, formatted and sent camera-ready to the printer for reproduction. In a company where thousands of employees are involved, the production of a telephone directory is an undertaking that word processing can greatly facilitate.

Decision support systems will increasingly find their way into the banks' executive suites, as they become more acceptable to the business environment. Forecast modeling, economic projections, including the graphics that are a part of these systems, make them very attractive to officers of financial institutions who need to keep a close watch, daily, on the fluctuations of the economy.

The Small Retail
or Wholesale Business

Many of the smaller retail or wholesale companies benefit from office automation by having multi-functional terminals that do both data and word processing for them. Among the direct applications they use are:

1. Simple correspondence, such as general letters, business and sales letters, collection letters, and perhaps short memoranda with the company.
2. Inventory control, such as pipe fittings for the plumbing supplies company; food for the caterer or restaurateur; chemicals for a research laboratory; and books for the bookstore. Computerized record keeping, as it relates to inventory and computerized ordering of supplies direct from a vendor who has equipment with which you can telecommunicate, is a critical time saver and a most efficient way for the small business to handle its inventory.

3. Accounting functions, such as accounts payable, receivables, general ledger, and payroll, are all obvious tasks of every business that need the efficiency and accuracy of automation.

Public Relations

Public relations departments in large and small companies are finding that word processing is essential to their function as the purveyors of images and the consumers of words. Even a simple, inexpensive word processor, in a public relations department, can perform such functions as electronically recording the text of a speech, article, release, report, or letter, and from the recorded text, run off several identical typescripts, each as an "original." Corrections can be made on the recorded text by merely typing in the corrections and outputting a fresh copy. A number of letters or releases can be produced, each containing slightly different texts and each an "original." With word processing, once the main text is recorded, only the material that changes from one version to another has to be keyboarded.

Copy for newsletters, brochures, and annual reports can all be typed and sent via telecommunications to a photocomposition machine. With the appropriate communication devices, a word processor can transmit from one office to another over telephone lines, and can access information from massive computerized data banks.

As business graphics capabilities are expanded, much of the artwork for these publications will be done on a computer, and also sent via communications lines to the typesetter, and ultimately to the printer for final reproduction.

Publishing

Word processing is a natural complement to lengthy manuscripts that must go through several revisions, edits, and rekeyboarding. Many publishers are beginning to see the importance of word processing technology as they encourage their authors to utilize microcomputers to input the original manuscript, which can then be edited on a screen and resubmitted to the author for corrections and additions. This same manuscript can also be sent via telecommunications directly to the typesetter without rekeyboarding.

Book editors now spending 40–60 percent of their time performing such rote tasks as copyediting and marking copy, reading and correcting proofs, compiling front and back matter, trafficking the flow of paper, and arranging for typing and retyping of drafts, will find that their attention can now be devoted to the more important creative tasks of seeking out new authors, and conducting market research studies to discover what types of books the public wants. By eliminating the duplication of keyboarding a manuscript at a typesetter's work station, the publishing industry can save up to 70 percent of a book's manufacturing cost.

Insurance

Insurance companies, too, are large users of words as part of their trade. One large insurance company that specializes in automobile insurance and personal accounts purchased a single standalone, as its first piece of information processing equipment. (A large mainframe had been handling data processing for the company for many years.) Within six months, the success with which the word processor handled paperwork led the department to add six terminals, three printers and a central processor. Some of the applications for which the word processor is used include formatting the writing of letters sent to insurance representatives in fifty-two states; the preparation of a large manual, transmitted directly to phototypesetting equipment via a communications link, for distribution to every field office in the company; and the retrieval of information stored on disk that relates to customer inquiries.

Among the reasons why the managers in the company feel that word processing was readily accepted by the employees includes the fact that no employee was forced to switch from a typewriter to the word processor, but was "invited" to try the new equipment. The terminals are not assigned to any particular individuals but are available to anyone, and many persons rotate. No one sits at a terminal for more than two hours at a stretch.

One of the advantages of the system, according to the word processing manager, is that changes can now be made in a long report or proposal, without it being necessary for a secretary to retype the entire document. As a result, professionals are more willing to proof more carefully and work in last minute changes without feeling guilty about the need to tie up a secretary to do a job over again.

Several users have indicated that one of the greatest advantages of computers is the ability to write materials and store them on disk for retrieval later. With minor updates and corrections, these documents, or "shelf pieces," are instantly available. Specific examples of "shelf pieces" include executive speeches, business proposals, and promotional letters for annual sales and seasonal products. By building a file of shelf pieces, projects can be done when there is time, instead of in the middle of a busy period.

Medicine

Even in medical facilities, information processing has come to play a major role. In hospitals, information must be kept current and readily accessible. Ideally, in a hospital, information about every patient should be available at the mere press of a button by the doctors, nurses, technicians, and administrators. It has been estimated that over 20 percent of a hospital's budget is utilized in information processing. From the moment a patient enters a hospital the paperwork cycle begins. A record must be kept of every test administered, every pill taken, every visit by the physician, and every vital sign that is read. Slowly, but surely, computer terminals, strategically placed throughout the hospital, can help to eliminate much of the paperwork and some of the errors in the constant human recording of information.

Current experiments are taking place in various hospitals, using computers to diagnose puzzling ailments and disease. As more and more sophisticated software becomes available to the medical community, the use of computers for medical diagnosis as a backup to human diagnosis will become common.

The computer is also finding its way into the doctors' individual offices for such repetitive chores as billing, the storage of patient records, and the word processing of insurance documents that take up so much of a medical secretary's time. Offices equipped with workstations are able to enter a patient's name, address, medical history, and other pertinent information when that patient walks in the door. This record is continuously updated as that patient goes through the routines of health care. It is available to a doctor within seconds if the patient calls six months later with a question about medications or with a complaint.

Information processing will not only help the medical profession by alleviating the great paperwork burden placed upon it by the endless government and insurance forms that must be completed; it will also result in better overall medical care that does not have to rely on a physician's memory and the human error that goes into the constant re-recording of information.

The systems described are merely a first step in the long walk to complete integration of information systems. Although a reality in some offices, there are many nonusers who should take a closer look at the potential for their business to improve productivity and impact on "the bottom line."

PART TWO

IMPLEMENTING AN OFFICE SYSTEM

The promise of electronics is one thing and the actual applications of the technology to an individual business is quite another. For the first time in the history of business, the combination of an information explosion, and the complexity of the new technology, forces the office to take a look at itself and determine just what are the goals, the ideals, and the practicalities of doing business. Although the often repeated expression, the "bottom line," is the ultimate purpose of every business, there are many pathways to achieving this aim. In the 1980s, automation must be a part of the overall scheme if the business is to succeed. There are many considerations, once the decision has been made, to bring in office automation. Among them are:

Information Management—How is it currently achieved? How will it change?

Hardware—What type of a system do you need?

Software—What applications will suit the needs of the office? Where do the software packages come from?

Ergonomics—What are the human factors to be considered, when bringing in automation?

Databases—How do you form a database to handle your files? How do you access outside databases?

Legal Issues—What do you need to know to avoid problems in the future?

Chapter Four

Information Management

So you have decided to purchase a computer! How to distinguish from the array of gadgets and machinery available and find a system that will meet your individual needs is more than a small problem. Computer salesmen will bombard you and all their systems will sound terrific. The brochures and pamphlets that appear each day in the morning mail are also alluring, interesting, and convincing. You do not understand "bits," "bytes," "64K memory." You do not see much difference between a word processor with a screen and a small business computer terminal.

How to implement an office system that will provide you with the most computing power for the money and give you the elasticity and expandability that you will need over the next five years is no easy task. The first step is to take a good look at your business—a look more fundamental than studying mere transactions, and come to understand just what it is you are processing each day.

The world population is generating information at a rate of 70 billion new pieces each year. The ability to manage that information will be an essential ingredient for a successful business in the 1980s. Less than 15 percent of the information in a typical organization is automated. Information is a resource that needs to be managed just as efficiently as raw materials are resources that need to be managed. Enter office automation!

Before putting in an office system, a business must look at its information practices and review such functions as records keeping, filing, and text processing. Every business has numbered files of information. They are highly structured and need to be accessed in a certain way. Every business issues form letters, standard memorandum, weekly, monthly, and yearly reports. In every business proposals are written to create new projects and to fund ongoing ventures.

An information management study will provide a complete picture of paper processing—records keeping, files, text processing, data processing, and inventory. Because historical information is the cornerstone of improving the future operations of a business, an information management study will give the business an analysis of how things have been done in the past.

The information management study should be performed either by a team of individuals chosen from the workforce to engage in this study and to report back to the managers or executives of the company; or it can be performed by outside, impartial consultants who work with the employees to assess the company's current and future needs. In companies where ultimate expenditures for computer equipment will be above $10,000 the services of an outside consultant for a few thousand dollars is a worthwhile investment.

Some of the specific areas that an information management study should look at are:

- the kinds of documents typed in the office;
- the allocation of time to these tasks by secretaries, clerks, typists, and managers;
- copiers and the kinds and numbers of copies made in the office;
- mail that is received and sent by each person or department in the company and how that mail is distributed;
- opinions and attitudes of workers in the office regarding some of these activities;
- telephone calls; how many incoming and outgoing and how they are routed;
- how the accounting functions of the office are handled;
- who is handling what particular tasks—i.e., a breakdown of the organizational structure;
- the physical design of the office and the changes that would result with computer equipment in the environment;
- vendors and the kinds of systems they have to offer at particular price ranges;
- the volume of information to be input to the computer and the relative memory capacity of particular systems.

The information management study should provide indicators as to where productivity in a business has lagged.

One large manufacturer of microprocessors found that productivity was so low in his firm that he instituted a "productivity program" to

FIGURE 4–1 Information Management.

combat the problem. With a few simple changes in office procedures—cutting xerox copies; reducing the number of steps required to handle the hiring and firing of employees; simplifying the format of reimbursement of expense accounts; streamlining the handling of accounts receivable and payable, and the personnel records keeping of the company—a marked increase in productivity was evident. All this was done in an office where automation had been implemented.

The information management study might also include a survey of employees to obtain their opinions and attitudes toward automation. This is one way of involving the people in the office and making them feel that they are participating in the decisions related to the impending change.

SAMPLE EMPLOYEE SURVEY

Name _____

Location _____

Position/Job Title _____

Questions

1. Could you please break down your work day into the following activities and indicate how much time you allot to these tasks. Assume six working hours:

   Typing _____ minutes

   Telephone Usage _____ minutes

   Receiving calls _____ minutes

   Making calls _____ minutes

   Meetings _____ minutes

   Clerical Activities _____ minutes

   Retrieving information _____ minutes

   Filing information _____ minutes

   Reading mail _____ minutes

   Answering mail _____ minutes

Miscellaneous _____ minutes

    Preparing reports, budgets, etc. _____ minutes

    Filling out forms _____ minutes

    Xeroxing _____ minutes

    Other _____ minutes

2. Are you in favor of office automation?

    Yes? _____

    No? _____

3. Do you feel that a computer will help you become more efficient at your job?

    Yes? _____

    No? _____

    If so, please explain _____

_____

4. Please rank in order those chores where you feel a computer will help you the most.

    Typing _____

    Filing _____

    Mail _____

    Retrieving information _____

    Telephone time _____

    Meetings _____

5. Can a computer terminal be placed at your current workstation without inconvenience?

    Yes? _____

    No? _____

    If the answer is no, please indicate why _____

_____

6. Have you ever used a computer terminal?

    Yes? _____

    No? _____

7. Do you own a computer at home?

    Yes? _____

    No? _____

In addition to the specifics that will be answered by the employee survey, the information management study should attempt to answer the following concerns about overall information manipulation:

1. When is it impossible to get information in the office?
2. When is there too much information?
3. What information is missing?
4. What do I process, words or data?
5. Who is going to use a computer?
6. How many people in the office will need terminals?

The results of this study must be compiled into a *written* report that will be a reference every step of the way toward automating an office.

Chapter Five

Hardware

All computer systems have a basic hardware configuration consisting of a central processor, a video display terminal, a keyboard, the main memory or information storage component, and the disk for holding the software programs and the data. In addition, almost every computer workstation has a printer to produce hard copy.

Beyond that there is a great diversity in size, shape, and price of computer systems. Computers range in size from the small personal computer with a general storage capacity of 16K and a price tag of between $2,000-$6,000; to the standalone systems with storage capacity of 64K up and price tags of between $6,000-$15,000; to larger systems ranging in size from 64K to unlimited memory capacity and in price from $20,000-$150,000.

STANDALONE

The term standalone information processor connotes a single total entity that includes the processor, keyboard, display screen, and printer. The memory and storage capacity of this type of system are limited to the capabilities of the processor. Standalone systems can be connected to other standalone systems via telecommunication lines. They usually can be up-

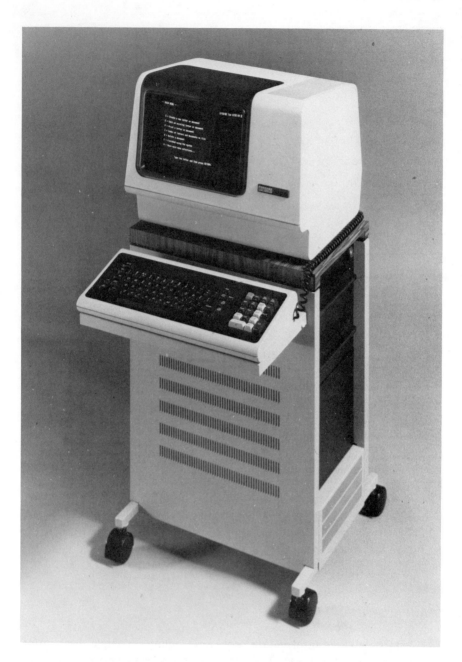

FIGURE 5-1 The DECmate Work Processor is a multifunction standalone system which offers a wide range of word processing operations inlcuding list processing, math, sort, and many data processing capabilities including accounts receivable and payable, payroll, general ledger and many business functions such as financial modeling.

graded to a more powerful computer and include in a multi-terminal configuration. Examples of standalone terminals include the Wangwriter, IBM Displaywriter, Infowriter by Honeywell Information Systems, the MICOM 2001, Lanier's EZ-1, and the DECmate. The personal computers are also standalones.

MULTI-TERMINAL

Multi-terminal systems, as the title suggests, are configurations that incorporate more than one workstation linked to a central processing unit. There are many different types of multi-terminal systems:

1. *Shared Logic Systems*, where a number of workstations share the logic, storage, and peripherals of a central computer.
2. *Clustered Multi-terminal Systems*, which support a small number of workstations and can consist of a combination of standalone terminals and "dumb" terminals linked to a central processing unit.
3. *Shared Resources Systems*, where each workstation contains its own intelligence and processing power, and the system is tied together merely by the information that can be shared among the terminals if desired.

Shared logic systems consist of one or more terminals, either with or without display screen, that are attached to a central processing unit (CPU). The terminals share disks and tape storage, and are able to communicate with one another. Printers and optical character readers can be attached to the same CPU and work within the system. A shared logic system can tolerate a high-speed printer for draft copy and low-speed printers for fine letter quality. With this configuration a cluster of operators can share the central processing capability. Shared logic systems can be set up with a minimum of two terminals.

As many as sixty terminals can be added. Shared logic systems are ideal in a larger environment where it may be desirable to share the work files among many operators and share the peripheral devices, such as a combination of letter-quality printers and high-speed printers.

Clustered systems usually support a smaller number of terminals or workstations than the shared logic systems and consist of a combination of standalone word processing terminals, complete with their own intelligence, disk drives, and terminals with little or no intelligence, that tie into one main system. A distinct advantage of the cluster system is the continuation of operation in times of a system breakdown. In a shared logic system if the main CPU is inoperable then all the equipment is rendered inoperable. In the cluster system if the main CPU is not working, the standalone units, which are merely tapping into the larger memory, can still function.

FIGURE 5-2 The Nixdorf 8840/5 is a shared resource word processing system. It features word wraparound, hyphenation scan, paragraph assembly, simultaneous input/output, merge of standard text with variables, diskette and/or mag tap archiving, and much more.

In a shared resource system, each workstation contains its own intelligence and processing power. Although the system appears to be very similar to the shared logic system, intelligence is dispersed rather than centralized. The shared resource system offers greater integrity and potential for continued operation than the shared logic system because each unit is entirely independent of other units and simply shares information.

All the multi-terminal or cluster systems encourage sharing of information and data, and encourage the automation of many administrative tasks, including calendar management, files, electronic mail, and list/record processing. The multi-functionality of the integrated terminals permits a combination of uses and may remove some of the limitations that apply to standalone systems.

The price tag for these multi-terminal systems ranges from $25,000 to over $150,000. Per station cost is usually between $10,000–$20,000. In the office that has need of two workstations it would be overkill to purchase a

FIGURE 5-3 Office Information Systems Address the Full Range of Word and Data Processing Tasks in Any Environment. An expanded version of the successful Wang word processing line, the Office Information System (OIS) family incorporates much of the leading-edge technology of Wang computers. The design of the OIS series means that each system performs more than advanced text processing. The powerful capabilities of every Office Information System allow sophisticated applications, to further improve productivity. Equally important, the OIS controls the most critical resource in any office—information.

shared system that can add up to 15 or 20 terminals. The office that envisions the possibility of ten or more individuals using terminals would not want to utilize standalones. Examples of shared systems include the Wang OIS and VS systems, the IBM 5520 series, NBI System 8 & 64, and many others.

Most computer systems developed since 1980 are combination data processing and word processing systems. If a particular configuration required by an office needs to include both word and data processing, it is important to determine if files require reformatting when data processing information is accessed through the word processing software and vice versa. Normal computing languages are used on these WP/DP multi-function terminals or systems and can include all the familiar machine languages, such as BASIC, FORTRAN, COBOL, and Pascal. Terminals that are primarily designed for data processing offer more complex mathematical capability than do many of the word processing systems that offer some minimal amount of data processing functionality.

Hardware considerations must include a decision as to the need for a system that is primarily for data processing with word processing software or the need for word processing capability with some basic data processing functions. The strength of a particular machine lies in one area or the other.

Among the familiar names in word processing are:

Word Processing

A.B. Dick	Lexitron Corporation
Basic Four	NBI Inc.
Burroughs	Olivetti
Compucorp	Philips Information Systems
CPT Corporation	Royal Business Machines
Dictaphone Corporation	Savin
Digital Equipment Corporation	Syntrex Inc.
Exxon Information Systems	Wang Laboratories
Four Phase Systems	Wordplex
IBM	Xerox
Lanier Business Products	

Data processing companies include:

Data Processing

Burroughs Corporation	Wang Laboratories
Digital Equipment Corporation	Nixdorf Corporation
NCR	Microdata
Basic Four	Quantel
Data General	Cado
Datapoint Corporation	Univac
Hewlett Packard	Prime Computer
Honeywell Information Systems	Shastra General Products
IBM	Texas Instruments

Several Japanese companies making inroads in the office automation market include:

Canon	
Casio	Mitsubishi
Hitachi	Toshiba Electric
Fujitsu	NEC Epson
Matsusshita	Tokyo Juki Industries

These lists are by no means complete and represent only a few of the vendors who can provide good equipment to a business at competitive prices.

FIGURE 5-4 The Nixdorf 8870 is a business computer that offers a building block approach to an office system. As your business expands, your computer will grow right along with you. Nixdorf offers several tailored business programs to match the way you do things. These programs cover a wide range of applications: mortgage closing, wholesale distribution, insurance agency management, client accounting, contractor management, and many others.

SMALL BUSINESS COMPUTERS

The small business computer is a tool for handling such functions as accounts receivable, accounts payable, payroll, update tracking of inventory, and general ledger. It is a software-based machine that is relatively easy for the first-time user to operate, and can be found in the standalone unit or as a component of a larger distributed data processing network.

The Yankee Group defines the small business computer as a computer "which derives its power from a programmable microprocessor, priced from $10,000, and is used to solve at least one business problem." This machine, says the Yankee Group, should be practical for the first-time user to install and should not require the services of a programme consultant.

A Yankee Group survey of small business computer users found that these machines were being used chiefly for "bookkeeping functions."

Small companies make use of all the basic applications of their small business computers—notably accounts receivable, and invoice/billing—whereas large companies use them for more sophisticated, tailored applications, such as communicating with other computers in the company and the solving of a business problem." (Yankee Group Industry Research Report, September, 1980.)

Most small business computers are capable of handling simple word processing tasks if they have the appropriate software packages. As users become more sophisticated in their needs, their demands for services will increase, and they will want their small business computers to be capable of handling graphics as well.

PRINTERS

Offices are a long way from becoming "paperless," and most tasks require hard copy output. Thus, printers are an essential part of almost every computer system.

Printers have not changed much since the early 1970s, when the daisy wheel was introduced by Diablo. The daisy wheel is a flat, rotating wheel with 96 characters perched at the ends of flexible reinforced nylon petals. It is an impact printer, which means that the characters are printed out by striking an inked ribbon that leaves a pattern on the paper. Although there

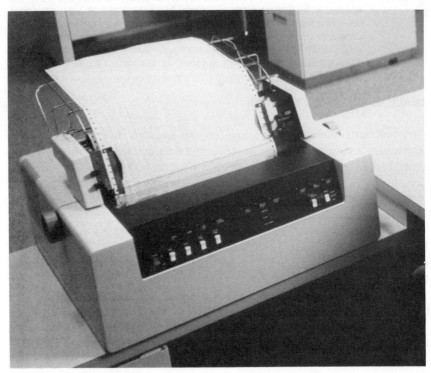

FIGURE 5-5 IBM Printer.

are several other impact printers on the market, the daisy wheel is the type sold with most small business or word processing systems.

When considering the purchase of a printer, decide whether or not a draft quality (high speed) or letter quality (lower speed) printer is appropriate. Many offices need both.

Printers are an important facet of the computer system and are often the component that can cause the most trouble to the user. Although printer technology is still in its infancy, there are several exciting technological developments that bear watching, including laser printing and fiber optics.

DISKS

Most smaller computer systems, particularly standalone word processing systems, utilize the 5¼- or 8-inch floppy disks as the primary storage medium. For systems requiring greater storage and flexibility, hard (rigid) disks are available. The user should understand that floppy disks are not at all similar in their design and thus are *NOT compatible* from one machine to another. The differences include the number of bits stored per inch (recording density) on the disk; the number of tracks per inch, and the number of sides on which data are recorded. Incompatibility between systems can also be from the way a system formats a disk, and locates system and directory tracks. The various categories of disks include:

1. Single density, single sided floppy diskette, where the data is written on one side only, leaving the opposite side completely empty.
2. Double density, single sided floppy diskette, which still uses only one side for recording data, but each sector recorded is twice the original density, allowing for more characters or bits/inch.
3. Single density, double-sided, floppy diskette, which allows information to be recorded on both sides of the diskette.
4. Double density, double-sided diskette, recording on both sides of the diskette, with the maximum number of characters on each side.
5. Rigid, hard, or micro Winchester memory disks. Their primary attraction is their vast storage capacity, up to 10 million bytes of memory (a byte is equivalent to a character), or the equivalent of three large novels.

Most of the word processing standalones use the 8-inch floppy diskette, which can store up to 1 million plus characters, with double density and double sides. The smaller personal computers generally use 5¼-inch floppy disks.

An individual selecting a computer system does not need to get too caught up with the intricacies of disk design, except to understand just how much storage he/she is going to get in relation to his/her particular needs.

The floppy disks have the important quality of removability from the system, whereas the rigid disks have far greater storage. It is important to realize how much bulk text has to be stored on a continuing basis. The other consideration is the ability of the computer system to upgrade to hard disk, which would provide greatly expanded storage capacity.

THE ROLE OF OCR

Optical character readers (or scanners) are machines that are capable of taking a page of typed copy, which has been keyboarded on a standard electric typewriter, and converting that copy to machine readable characters that can be automatically input to a word processor. Most OCRs can read all common type fonts. The role of the OCR has been hotly debated. Some have felt that if word processors are justified through the productivity increases and cost savings they incur, then an OCR, which will speed up the process of inputting material to the word processor, should be that much more efficient and effective. OCR proponents say that with an OCR, the word processor becomes an extension of all the typewriters in an organization, eliminating time-consuming retyping and allowing the word processors to concentrate on their primary function of editing and correcting.

When an office first purchases word processing and is in the throes of inputting all of its files to form its database, OCR is more than a helpful aid. Once the database has been established, however, there is a question as to how valuable this rather expensive machine will be. Most OCR units sell for upwards of $18,000. OCR services can be rented through certain companies, such as Kurzweil, for a more reasonable fee.

In certain industries or professions, there is no question about the value of OCR capability. In law firms, for instance, with their voluminous reams of paperwork, which for many years to come will be generated mostly on typewriters, OCR capability is, indeed, an asset. The OCR takes no more than five minutes to read a document into a word processing system, while it takes a typist hours to type the same document into the system.

In publishing, where authors' manuscripts are usually submitted typed, OCR is of great assistance. It is also useful to groups or institutions that are creating databases of previously published materials, and to publishers of newspapers and magazines who deal with volumes of written materials daily. Many successful examples of OCR use have been cited.

One engineering company that issues reports consisting of many thousands of pages of specifications, with complicated mathematical formulas and Greek symbols, has found that by using word processing with an OCR, they experienced a drop in the time required to produce their reports from 10–12 days to 1–2 days. The OCR, in this case, reduced keyboarding requirements by one full-time person. Their annual savings with the automated equipment has been many thousands of dollars—significantly more savings than the cost of the initial hardware.

When word processors become a fixture of every desk in the office, the OCR will lose its usefulness. At this point there will not be any rekeyboarding. Document generation will be done directly on a terminal by the originator of the document. Until that time, OCR should be considered when the hardware purchase process is about to begin.

FIGURE 5–6 Kurzweil OCR.

COMPUTER SYSTEM
SUPPLIERS

Retail Outlet

There are several ways in which a buyer may purchase computer equipment. He may go into a retail outlet and buy a computer system, just as he goes into an automobile dealership and purchases a car. While at the retail store, he may walk around and look at various pieces of equipment, pick out those features and options that appeal to him, pack the equipment into his car, and take it home. Service on such a purchase is done via an 800 toll-free telephone number, or through a service contract purchased at the time that the equipment is bought. Training to use such equipment is provided through a self-paced manual that is supplied with the equipment at the time of the purchase.

The simplicity of taking a machine off the shelf in a store and plugging it into a wall outlet is fine for the home user or hobbyist. For a businessman it can be a risky way to purchase his equipment. The terminal, which is intended to help the business increase its productivity and alleviate the paperwork in the office so that the business will run more efficiently, should be purchased with care, consideration, and more assurances than can be provided by the retail outlet. A fairly complicated process of analysis and study must be undertaken before a system is purchased. A continuing process of monitoring a system needs the expertise of a vendor who knows the system. Unless the businessman is familiar with computers and knows exactly what his needs are and how they can be met, buying anything but a small personal computer from a retail outlet is usually unwise.

Direct from Vendor

The second way that a user can purchase computer equipment is directly from a vendor through the local sales representatives. Most sales representatives are willing to give an extensive presentation on the various systems that they have to offer, and to explain the advantages and disadvantages of each system. If the proper information management study has been done, working with various vendors is easy. As a general rule, a user should interview at least three or four established vendors who have systems with the capabilities that he has determined will be needed. It is important to be sure that the vendors have been in business a long time and have a good reputation regarding the particular equipment that the business is purchasing. Many of the established companies are stronger in either word processing, data processing, or distributed data processing, and those strengths should be well understood. The financial stability of a vendor company also has to be considered. A purchaser wants to make sure that the company from whom he is buying his equipment is able to support that equipment with the proper service organization. He also wants to make sure that the company has a planned program for training people in how to use the equipment. The training manual has to be reviewed for clarity and legibility. If the training manual cannot be understood, people will not understand how to use the equipment.

When purchasing hardware it is essential that the buyer is knowledgeable about the memory capacity of the equipment, the on line storage capability, and whether or not that memory capacity is large enough to handle the workload. It is also important to consider the equipment's expandability, compatibility with other pieces of equipment, and possible links to other networks and communication facilities.

OEM

A third way that a buyer can purchase equipment is from an OEM. The initial OEM stands for "Original Equipment Manufacturer." Actually, the acronym is a misnomer, because the OEM generally is not the original manufacturer, but is a company that purchases component parts from various manufacturers. The OEM puts these pieces together into a highly customized, sophisticated system, which he provides along with the appropriate software to the user who has special applications needs.

The Dealer/Distributor

Another source for computer equipment is through dealers or distributors who serve as sales representatives for one or more vendors. Generally, these dealers will also provide training and support for the system after it is installed. The danger in purchasing from these companies is that they may go out of business, or eliminate your computer system from their line of products several months or years after you have purchased the system, and you are left without the proper support.

Purchase Considerations

Before making a final decision on a system you need to have the following:

1. Detailed specifications of all pertinent hardware and software. This includes the memory and storage capacity of the computer; the types of printers that can be attached to the system; the types of disk utilized by the system, and whether or not the system can accommodate hard disk (expanded storage) with business growth. Software considerations include the list of applications packages available from the vendor that can operate on the system, and whether or not the computer can utilize packaged software now available, such as the CP/M software library (Control Program for Microprocessors). Consider too

whether or not communications is available and at what cost, including the cost of modems.

2. A written proposal, stating exactly what equipment—software, peripherals— is being purchased for exactly what amount of money. Specific explanations of the technical support and training programs needed should be included in this proposal, as well as a projected delivery date of the system.

3. A full-scale demonstration of the equipment you are planning to purchase should be offered by the vendor, using one of your own applications, so that you can evaluate the system's processing speed, clarity, and ease of use.

4. A list of users in your area that have the system should be made available to you by the vendor, so that you can talk with them about the system's function and reliability.

5. An understanding of physical space requirements, including the need for new furniture, cable, electrical outlets, lighting and air conditioning.

PURCHASE, RENT OR LEASE?

One of the major considerations when looking at computer systems is whether you should purchase the equipment outright from the vendor or rent / lease it.

There are two leasing arrangements offered by most vendors—monthly rental or a three to five year leasing arrangement. Both are tax deductible.

Although the long range cost of the equipment is greater to the consumer who leases or rents his equipment, there are valid reasons why not purchasing is sometimes desirable.

Rentals

Because the technology is rapidly changing, newer, faster, more efficient models are coming out each year. The business that rents equipment has the option to continuously upgrade without additional cost. Service, too, is usually included in a piece of equipment that is owned by the vendor. For a business anticipating unusual growth or a radical change in business operations, it would be advantageous to rent rather than buy equipment outright.

Leasing

Leases are usually negotiated for a three- or five-year period. They are not as flexible as rental arrangements and do not include the option to change to newer equipment as it comes on the market. Usually with a leasing arrangement, the lessor must pay a service contract fee for maintenance of the equipment. The advantages of the leasing arrangement over the rental plan include the lower premiums paid over the longer term and the ability of the user leasing equipment to purchase that equipment at the end of the leasing term, usually for an additional surcharge.

Usually the decision whether or not to rent, lease, or purchase is based on two factors: the availability of cash to pay for a system outright and various tax considerations. A businessman who purchases equipment, under the current laws (Economic Recovery Tax Act of 1981), is given a direct 10 percent reduction on income taxes against the purchase price of equipment. Thus, if the computer cost $1,000, the taxes would automatically be reduced by $100 in the year that the equipment was purchased. The buyer is also allowed an annual depreciation on equipment, and that is spread over a five-year period for most computer equipment.

With a leasing arrangement, an investment tax credit may or may not be passed from the vendor to the purchaser. That decision should affect the lease payment when it is negotiated between the vendor and the user.

With a rental, 100 percent of the rental fee is deductible as a business expense.

There are no hard and fast rules regarding the question of purchase versus lease—each case must be deliberated individually.

The bottom line, when reviewing the implementation of an office system, is what it will do for you today and what it can do for your business tomorrow. Hardware expandability is a must. The computer system should accept peripheral equipment, such as printers and disks, which are essential. The same system in other applications might need to be expanded to accept speech recognition capabilities, greater memory capacity, and an interface with a larger network or database that the business might have to access. Choosing the hardware is not easy, but the toughest part—making the system work for you in an efficient, cost effective manner—is ahead. If the initial hardware considerations are thorough however, the job ahead will be a lot simpler.

Chapter Six

Software

"The computer is no better than its program," wrote Elting Elmore Morison in a book entitled *Man, Machines and Modern Times*, 1966.

The program he referred to, also known as the computer's software, is what makes the machine "tick."

Computers are dumb and inanimate. They have to be told, in agonizing detail, exactly what steps to perform, and when and how to perform them, by an intelligent source who is capable of turning their raw power into useful applications.

Software is the term the computer industry has coined for the instructions that go into the machine to make it work. It is in the software that the computer system user will see differences among systems. It is up to the software programmed into the computer to determine how that machine will react and what it will do.

When the computer industry first began, the cost of the hardware was the significant factor in determining which system to purchase. Gradual improvements in the manufacture of hardware and the availability of cheaper and more powerful "chips," have dropped computer hardware costs significantly. Software costs have risen dramatically, as more and more programs have been developed to expand the capabilities of the computer beyond the wildest ideas of those early computer pioneers. It is generally agreed that, during the decade of the '80s, software costs will continue to rise above the cost of hardware, as more packages are designed to enable the user to accomplish more tasks.

For the newcomer to computer technology, understanding the difference between what is hardware and what is software is very difficult. Although a sophisticated understanding of the technical mechinations of software can be left to the programmer and to the engineer, there is a basic knowledge of software that any user should have.

SYSTEMS AND APPLICATIONS

There are two distinct categories of software in any computer system—the internal or operating software called "systems software," comprised of programs that control the execution of other programs and generally see that the hardware is operating efficiently; and the applications software, or the programs that enable the user to carry out specific chores.

Many of the capabilities of a computer system are the result of the operating software that supervises the overall function of the system and controls the flow of programs and data through the system. Operating software also serves to convert programming language instructions into machine language instructions; it enables the data in a computer to be arranged into a specific order and to be merged with other data.

Applications software are specific programs designed to allow the user of a computer to perform certain tasks. During the 1970s and early 1980s, applications programs were developed that can make the computer do almost everything from adding a simple column to analyzing a complex medical program, and presenting both a diagnosis and solution.

The need for software to do these and other complicated applications will increase during the 1980s. This new software will be "user dictated"— adapted to the quest of the modern nontechnical user to find a better and faster way to solve his business problems via automation. Users ask that their computers have multifunction capability, so that they can be used as both a small business computer and a word processor. They want their terminals to have graphics capability as well. The technology is progressing at such a rapid pace that these user-dictated demands will be met through software-based systems. In other words, it is the programs that are put into the computer that will determine the functions of the computer, and not the design and structure of the hardware itself.

Datapro, a market research corporation in the high technology field, has published a report identifying twelve areas of specific software applications that will be prominent throughout the 1980s. The twelve areas include: accounting; banking and financing; education; engineering; scientific;

insurance; management sciences; manufacturing; mathematics and statistics; medical and health care; payroll and personnel; sales and distribution; and word processing.

Datapro research indicates that the 1980s will see a steady and continued growth in accounting packages to meet increasing paperwork requirements at both the Federal and State levels. They see a growing demand for manufacturing control systems and project planning programs. Banking software will be needed as the banking community expands its electronic funds transfer and automated teller capabilities. Software applications for the medical and health services environment and applications for scientific purposes, such as engineering and mathematical analysis, statistical analysis and forecasting, will be in high demand. New word processing will also be needed to allow expanded systems to include such features as electronic mail and links to networks.

Inexpensive software packages to help prepare income taxes, keep track of household budgets, and address the needs of the expanding home computer market, will continue to proliferate as the hardware for home computers continues to drop in price (*Datapro Directory of Software,* Datapro Research Corporation, 1981).

Software is being written that will "manage" the applications a particular company already has on line. For example, one company wrote a data dictionary to provide a key to where all computer data is located. This is an attempt to capture and store, in a central location, all data utilization and documentation for purposes of control and flow. Vendors are now putting into their software application packages word dictionaries, spelling guides, punctuation, and grammar, to help the software of a particular system identify and correct errors that are input when a document is created. There is even software being written that will help the computer diagnose its own ills and determine the correct remedy to solve the malfunction.

When a new user is investigating the various systems that are available to meet his needs, he tends to get caught up with the hardware vendor's presales enthusiasm for a system. Software, at this stage of the game, becomes a secondary concern to the design and functionality of the hardware within a particular office structure. It is important for users to be aware of the costs of ownership and to understand that, in the average computer installation, more of their money will be spent on the development, maintenance, and add-on purchase of software than on hardware, over the life of the computer system. It is also important for new users to understand that in many cases, the applications software purchased with a system will only meet 80 percent of their overall needs. Research has shown that in a majority of applications there is 20 percent of unmet needs in the initial software purchases that must be made up in the future, either by looking for additional packaged software, by employing the skills of an in-house programmer, or by seeking a software consultant to prepare a program to customize the needs of the business to the functionality of the computer system.

WHERE TO FIND
THE SOFTWARE

There are many sources of supply for basic computer software that are available to a user.

Hardware Vendors

Most computer software has traditionally been sold to the user, at least during the initial purchase, by the equipment manufacturers. Potential users look at what they consider to be complete systems, which include both the hardware and the software provided by the vendor. The important fact for a user to remember is that hardware vendors are intent on selling them a system, and put more emphasis on the design of their machines than on the software needs of the individual customer. It is important to separate hardware and software, in your own mind, and determine the best software for your particular needs.

New users also have to be aware that computer makers will often design more software, which requires additional storage and / or peripheral equipment, than may be needed to accomplish their applications. Separating hardware and software needs, and determining the necessary configuration for a particular application requires careful study and consideration.

Independent Software Suppliers

Software houses have grown like "topsy" in recent years and promise to continue to grow even more over the next several years. Because in-house programmers are difficult to find and expensive to keep, many companies have turned to software houses for the customized programs that they need. Many of these software companies have also developed "mass marketed" software packages that are cost efficient and designed to meet a variety of needs. More of these mass produced packages will come on the market as the technology advances.

Standard software has the same disadvantage as does any standard product—it is not an exact fit and requires the user to modify his business practice. However, it does provide the user, especially the small user, with a way to automate such relatively simple business tasks as text entry, accounting, payroll, general ledger, order entry, and inventory.

During the 1980s "user friendly" or easy-to-use software, utilizing English commands, which require no knowledge of programming languages, will expand in the market. These systems will not only help users learn how to cope with their systems more easily, but will enable them eventually to customize their own programs without any specific knowledge of programming techniques or languages. Market analysts predict that completely user friendly systems are several years from reality.

In-House Development of Software

Among large companies most applications software has been written by a staff of employees hired for that purpose. As these companies expand their information processing capabilities, they turn to distributed data processing, which brings computing power to all departments and all employees and takes it out of the hands of the data processing professionals. Skyrocketing costs, missed deadlines, and the inability of companies to hire capable personnel to fill software needs, has led many to look to outside sources for their software. These large corporations have realized that it is nearly 10 times cheaper to purchase ready-made packages than it is to develop a package in-house. Although the ready-made packages have their shortcomings, they can be as reliable as the in-house packages in their rough stages.

In the office of the future, in-house development will continue in the large corporation. However, the programming staff will spend more time on modifying packaged programs than on developing new programs.

Computer Stores

In major metropolitan areas, computer stores can be found on nearly every block. These stores sell computer systems right off the shelf, and have a large selection of software programs available to meet many needs. It sounds easy and attractive, but buyer beware! The software found in computer stores is fine for the home hobbyist and, in some cases, for the user who has basic business applications to which he will apply his systems. This software usually comes with no warranty. Generally it will meet a need *only* when a customized program is not necessary.

Computer stores will continue to grow and to expand their software libraries. As users become more sophisticated, they will be able to take advantage of software packages marketed in these stores and customize them for their individual needs. In the initial stages of purchase, however, users should not be swayed by the apparent ease with which a purchase can be made, the line of supermarket packaging, or the promise of lower prices.

Miscellaneous Other Sources for Computer Software

User Groups. Several computer user groups have formed in major metropolitan areas. These groups develop software programs and provide them free to their members. Unfortunately these programs can be of a poor quality and support for them is usually nonexistent.

Software Brokers. Companies acting as intermediaries between software developers and buyers are software brokers. For the user who has specific needs and cannot fulfill those needs in the general marketplace, the software broker may fill the gap. The user must be aware that not all brokers are fully staffed to install, support, and maintain the packages they sell.

Turnkey System Suppliers. A number of companies purchase computers and peripheral equipment and then develop the necessary software to supply a complete system to a particular end user. This avenue for obtaining software is particularly attractive to the user who has had little or no experience in dealing with the technicalities of computers. Turnkey system suppliers provide customized systems for special needs. The reliability of a turnkey system supplier must be checked, because any system will require support and maintenance after a purchase has been made, and it is important to know that the supplier of the equipment will be available in future months and years to render needed services.

Universities are also working hard to develop software that they are offering for sale. Remember that most university packages are related to research, and that the support and enhancements that are necessary after the initial purchase may not be forthcoming from a university supplier.

Although the technology of basic circuitry is fine-tuned to such a point that a tiny speck of a chip can now do what it used to take a large room full of equipment to do; it is the limitations of the software programmer that will hold the industry back. Market researchers predict that the need for programmers could reach 1.5 million by 1990, more than triple the number working in 1980, bearing major changes in software technology. Users must be made aware that they may have fancy hardware sitting on their desks that has a capability that may never be fulfilled, owing to a lack of software.

LEGAL SNAGS

Other issues developing in the software industry involve the questions of software taxation and software copyright.

More than 27 state governments have recently passed laws mandating that a sales tax will be imposed on computer software, just as it is imposed on other tangible property. This means that when computer users buy pre-written, packaged software they will pay a sales tax. Some custom programs, however, are not taxed whereas others are, depending upon how they are sold. There is a controversy over whether or not computer timesharing services should be subject to this tax.

The Federal government views software as intangible and therefore not taxable. It is obvious that the issue is far from settled, and will be discussed further in the 1980s.

The other legal issue involves the question of copyright of software programs. In an historic decision in 1980, a court in England ruled in favor of the allowing microcomputer software copyright. The case of *Molimerx* v. *Kansas City*, has led U.S. industry analysts to review the issue of copyright of software, and this question is bound to be addressed in court cases in the future.

FINDING THE RIGHT SOFTWARE

Finding the right software package from the right source, which is compatible with the right equipment, is no easy task for the user, especially the user who is not familiar with the technology. In a report included in the *Datapro Directory of Microcomputer Software, 1981*, the Datapro Research Corporation lists the following guidelines, which merit careful attention:

1. Does the package meet overall basic needs?
2. Will the package run successfully on your particular computer system? Will it run at peak efficiency?
3. Is the applications package one that will adapt to the systems programming that is in your computer?
4. Is the package flexible? Does it accommodate to the changing requirements of your business? Does it have expandibility?
5. How difficult will it be to install the package? Will it require specialized documentation?
6. Will the package be easy to use? Is adequate documentation provided with the package?
7. What support will the software vendor provide?
8. Who are the other users of this software and how do they feel about it?
9. How long has this system been operational? Are all the "bugs" and "snags" out of the system?
10. What is the cost of acquiring and using the software package?

The Datapro Directory also listed a ten-step acquisition procedure for software packages that users should need:

1. Determine the requirements.
2. Gather information about the available package.
3. Narrow the field by rejecting unsuitable packages.
4. Perform a detailed evaluation and comparison for "factors to evaluate."
5. Talk to users.

6. Conduct benchmark tests.
7. Make the decision.
8. Negotiate a sound contract.
9. Install the package.
10. Check the results.

(*Datapro Directory of Microcomputer Software,* 1981, Datapro Research Corp.)

*   *   *

Good applications software will be no guarantee for good management. Whatever the size and sophistication of a particular office, the computer system, with its software, will not provide an answer to all office problems. It will only serve as a means to more efficient business operations. As is evident from the previous discussion, the understanding, acquisition, and ultimate utilization of software is a complex procedure with many variables, and many questions that the technology itself has not yet addressed. The industry seems to be intent on "reinventing the wheel" each time another vendor prepares a software package that is almost identical in design and function to one that is already available. Standardization must take place in this technology if the office of the future is to be a better, more efficient workplace than is the office of the '80s. A programmer shortage will plague the industry for the remainder of the century. Software must not only become standardized but it must be portable as more and more users become involved in the computer industry and begin to upgrade and trade in old systems for newer, better, and faster equipment.

Chapter Seven

Ergonomics

The most successful offices to have implemented automation have looked not only at the mechanics of the computer hardware, the effectiveness of computer software, the emotional and psychological impact of the systems as they relate to people, but also at the physical design of the workstation, as it fits into the total office environment.

The traditional office was patterned after a library or a study, with the executive or manager closeted within an elegantly paneled room, where he could study, read, and meditate. The secretary sat just outside the door of this office ready to execute commands.

Today management concepts have changed, and the demands of modern decision making include an ongoing communication process with an open and free interchange of ideas. Offices contain an informality and ease in the working environment. They have opened up, not only among the people themselves, but in the way in which they are designed to accommodate this new psychology. Automation has played no small role in affecting these changes.

Ergonomics, or the study of the interface of man and machine, is a relatively new science devoted to looking at the most effective design of a workstation and its placement in the office environment. Concerns about the physical and psychological impact of video display terminal use emanated originally, not from the United States labor force, but from Europe. Throughout the 1970s, groups in many European countries conducted extensive studies related to the questions of eyestrain, backache, muscular problems, and other physical stress encountered by VDT operators. Their findings led to a change in the design of computer terminals introduced during the late 1970s and early 1980s. Computer buyers began to see workstations with removable keyboards and tiltable screens. Terminals now had a special finish on the screen to eliminate glare and eyestrain. Custom designed worktables, and chairs curved to accommodate even the most sensitive backs were sold with many systems. The bulky machines that had been used were beginning to disappear.

In the United States a study of the ergonomic design of video display terminals was conducted by the National Institute for Occupational Safety and Health (NIOSH), at the request of a consortium of labor unions. The NIOSH study focused on three areas:

1. Measurement of illumination and luminance levels;
2. Measurement of the physical dimension of the workstation;
3. Direct observation of workstation features that were of special interest, including adjustability of screen contrast and brightness, adjustability of the chair, adjustability of the keyboard and screen position, and desk characteristics.

The results of all this attention to "ergonomics" has brought to the office workstations that are smaller, more compact, more flexible, and more adjustable. But this is not enough. The implementation of office automation must include an analysis of each employee's specific job function; his/her interaction with other employees and supervisors; his/her privacy needs; paper flow; traffic flow; noise levels—all in relation to the design and placement of the workstation in the overall office scheme.

According to a study conducted by The Buffalo Organization for Social and Technological Innovation (BOSTI), which attempted to look at the impact of the physical environment of office workers as it related to job satisfaction, most workers (70 percent) do not want a private office. About 40 percent indicated in the nationwide survey that they preferred working in an office with between one and seven persons. The remaining 30 percent stated that they preferred an office with more than seven workers. Other studies have shown that people who collaborate during the day should be clustered, using shorter panels that do not hinder communications. Where more privacy is required, taller panels can be used to separate employees. Sound privacy, essential to supervisors, is achieved by keeping supervisory offices slightly removed from other workstations. Smoked plexiglass panels encourage interaction between supervisors and employees without sacrificing sound privacy. Small enclosed conference rooms need to be available for times when closed door privacy is needed. In areas where equipment noise is a problem, such as the computer input area, custom designed acoustic panels help to minimize, but not eliminate, the problem.

There are several specific "ergonomic" issues that every office must consider before installing a computer system.

1. NOISE. The increasing acquisition by many offices of VDT equipment with associated printers and other telecommunications devices, in a setting that is not walled in, has resulted in high noise levels which are irritants to users and nonusers in the environment. This factor tends to reduce rather than increase productivity. The use of improved acoustical panels that absorb distracting sounds is one solution. Carpeting is another. Much of the noise comes from the printers, which can be covered to partially alleviate the problem. Future improvements in printer technology, hopefully, will provide further elimination of noise.

2. HEAT. Terminals emit heat. They must be placed in rooms that are air conditioned. Although the installation of special air conditioning units specifically for terminals is not usually necessary, a basic air conditioning system needs to be functioning year round.

3. ILLUMINATION. Research has shown that glare from improper lighting will affect the ability of a VDT operator to work. One solution is the use of lighting in the furniture itself to replace harsh overhead lights, which cause glare. Several furniture designers have lights mounted on

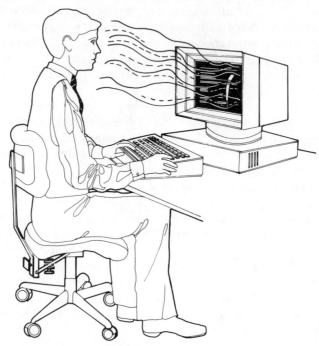

FIGURE 7-1   Ergonomics of Illumination.

structural panels and on the top of storage shelves that are a part of the work-station. Another solution is the use of tiltable and adjustable VDT screens, which are offered by some vendors, so that the operator is able to select an angle that is comfortable. Other considerations include recessed or louvered lighting or antireflection filters that fit over the screen.

4. OPTHOMOLOGICAL QUESTIONS. VDT operators have had problems associated with deterioration of visual acuity, headache, and burning eyes. Employers have to take responsibility for insuring that terminal operators, complaining of eye problems, have access to complete and competent opthalmological examination.

5. STATIC ELECTRICITY. VDT terminals tend to give off a lot of static electricity. So much, in fact, that it can become a problem for the operator, those in close contact with the operator, and for the terminal itself. There are several sprays on the market that help cut down on static electricity. If the problem persists there are also antistatic mats, placed beneath the work-station, that have proven to be an effective cure for this problem.

6. FURNITURE DESIGN. The chair is probably the most important aspect of user comfort, and increased productivity. Uncomfortable seating has been cited as the chief cause of backstrain, neckstrain, and headache

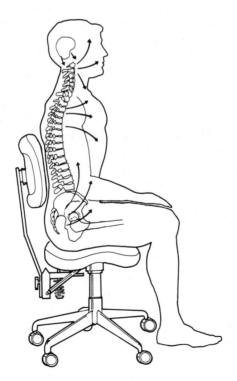

FIGURE 7-2 Ergonomics of Chair Design.

complaints so frequently voiced by clerical workers. Although it is impossible to build a chair for one person that will fit the physical dimensions of another, it is possible to provide adjustable furniture components to fit all sizes and shapes.

One of the ways to avoid problems after a computer system has been installed and an office has been rearranged to suit its new acquisition, is to involve people in the planning process before they are moved around like pawns on a chessboard. This can be done in the following ways:

1. Hold meetings to explain the objectives of a new office design, before moving even the smallest piece of furniture.
2. Ask the people who will be moved to offer their ideas and suggestions, possibly through a survey or an employee suggestion box. Once you ask for suggestions, review them carefully and try to incorporate as many as possible. Do so visibly, so that those involved will feel that their ideas are meaningful.
3. Do a good selling job. Embark on a public relations campaign to let your employees know that you are trying to enhance their jobs and increase the productivity of their work. Give them specific reasons and assurances why a change is good.
4. Draw a floorplan and post it so that everyone will know what is going to happen.

Chapter Eight

Legal Issues

The more laws and order are made prominent, the more thieves and robbers there will be.

Lau-tzu c. 604–531 B.C.
(Taken from *Bartletts Familiar Quotations,* John Bartlett)

The issue of office automation involves not only management concerns, but legal questions as well. When a new user investigates automation, he has to be aware of certain legal matters that he will have to address. He has to be aware that there have been court cases on computer issues and that there are laws affecting the pathways that technology will take in the future.

A hypothetical example of a prevalent type of case involving computers follows.

The XYZ Corporation, a business that purchased a computer system and relied on the system to do many functions, which would enhance its business and increase productivity, sues a vendor company for "overselling and misrepresentation." During the pre-sale discussions, the vendor's salesmen assured the XYZ Corporation that its system, above and beyond all others, would accomplish a list of tasks. The system has failed. Business loss has resulted, because XYZ has not been able to fulfill its promises to its customers—promises based upon its expectations of the computer's output. The crux of the problem with the computer was the system's slow response time; insufficient memory; general failure to perform multiprocessing functions as represented by the sales personnel. The malfunctions are blamed on both the hardware and the software.

Cases such as these have involved situations where, according to a user company, the system frequently, and without warning, erases a number of the company's primary and backup data files; the system wipes out entire accounts receivable and the backup disk; or it erases the current inventory files. Lost sales, lost profits, and punitive damages are sought after by the plaintiffs. Do they have a case?

NEGOTIATING THE CONTRACT

A user's first contact with legal questions arising from a computer purchase, is when he is faced with the prospect of signing the contracts to make the purchase. All too often, a business client will walk into his lawyer's office with a copy of a contract that he has already signed with a hardware or software vendor, anxious to file a suit because the system he has purchased is not performing to his expectations. He will discover that the contract he signed merely had some vague language about how the vendor agreed to provide certain equipment or services. The warranty that he thought he had on the equipment or software provides very few specific promises.

Computer vendors negotiate contracts for a living. Their marketing technique is designed to make contract signing swift, easy, and seemingly unimportant to the user—just a mere formality. Few buyers really know what to look for in the fine print of the computer contracts they sign. As a result, the contracts usually give the vendor much more protection than the buyer, and should be carefully reviewed by both the purchaser and his attorney before a signature is put on the dotted line.

Are these contracts negotiable? Anything is negotiable! Vendors are in the business of selling and they want to make a sale. Some points to question when reviewing a contract are:

1. *Delivery date.* A smart user will pin a vendor down to an approximate time frame for the delivery of a computer system. A clause should be included in the contract providing that for each day of delay on that delivery, *if your business would suffer loss,* you would be entitled to recover for that loss by an amount agreed upon by buyer and seller.

2. *Risk of loss.* Some computer contracts are written so that the buyer is responsible for the equipment from the time it leaves the manufacturer. This is unreasonable, and the buyer should be sure he is not responsible for equipment until it reaches his premises.

3. *The "merger" clause.* This clause states that the agreement between the customer and the vendor, as stated in the contract, is binding and is exclusive of any communication, such as an owner's manual, advertising literature, or oral promises made by the vendor to the buyer. It is a clause that buyers should attempt to eliminate from the contract. If this is not possible, the buyer should attempt to insert a specific statement indicating that other communications between the buyer and the vendor are binding as well, such as promotional literature.

4. *Liability clause.* Most contracts state that the purchaser has all liability for failure of the equipment to perform up to his expectations. This is the most important clause in the contract, because a buyer is putting much of his business into the system being purchased. If the system malfunctions and data is lost, or if repairs to the system are delayed and business loss results, the impact can be devastating to the financial well-being of the buyer's business. This is the area of contention in most legal suits, brought by buyers against vendor companies. A properly drawn contract (from the point of view of the buyer) will include a warranty clause, assuring the buyer of the right to expect certain standards in the system he is buying, and a certain level of performance by a vendor to make speedy repairs on a defect in the system.

Other specific contract provisions should include:

Environmental Requirements. Most computer hardware is designed to operate within a specific environment, including such factors as the availability of power outlets, heat and air conditioning, and space. If the vendor has assured the buyer that all the environmental requirements have been met for the successful implementation of a system, the user should not have to go to costly renovations when the system fails. If renovations are necessary, the vendor should point those out in advance.

Supplies. Most companies require supplies that meet certain specifications for a particular system. Those specifications must be clearly outlined in the contract, so that the buyer does not spend money procuring the wrong supplies only to find that he has damaged the system and must pay for costly repairs.

Upgrade, Trade In, Purchase Option. The ability of the purchaser to upgrade his system easily, to trade in the system for a newer model, or to purchase a system that is leased, should be clearly stated in the contract.

Maintenance. The type of maintenance, time and materials, response time to a repair call, and self-help provisions should be specifically written out in the contract, so there is no question in the minds of either the vendor or the purchaser, when a system is in trouble. The contract should also have a specific provision for the availability of loan equipment in the event the system is "down" for a long period of time.

There are several factors to be considered in providing routine maintenance for the system, including the cost of various types of maintenance via the service contract; travel and other expenses; how much notice does a user get before a rate charge in repair costs becomes effective; who supplies routine maintenance—i.e., engineers, installers, programmers, mechanics, etc.

In some cases a user may find it to be more economical to have maintenance done in-house or to have maintenance contracted out to a third party company, independent of the manufacturer. The precise arrangements concerning maintenance should be outlined in the contract because they impact on other aspects of the contract such as the liability clause.

Training. The contract should also delineate the areas of responsibility involved in the training of personnel to use the equipment. What training is provided to the buyer and at what charge (if any)? What training is the responsibility of the user? How many employees are included in the "free training program? Over what period of time is the training to be accomplished?

PURCHASE, LEASE, OR RENT?

The decision whether to buy, lease, or rent a computer system is one that is faced by everyone. Many factors enter into the final determination: fear of equipment obsolescence, the cost of money, tax and accounting considerations, and other economic and practical issues.

The decision should be based upon answers to the following questions:

1. How much money is available for a purchase, and what is the cost of borrowing money?
2. What are the tax considerations: federal, state, local, in the following areas:
   a. investment tax credit
   b. depreciation period
   c. sales tax
3. What will be the value of the system at the end of the lease?
4. What is generally best for the organization, regardless of the actual dollars?

TAXES

Several court cases have grappled with taxation questions in regard to computer use—both on hardware and software. The decisions so far have not resulted in any uniformity or clear cut guidelines for users. There needs to be an awareness that legal changes affecting the industry will occur in the future.

Currently, the Federal government regards software as intangible unless it is bundled (included with the price of the machine), when it can be treated as hardware. As a result the Federal government does not recognize taxes on software purchases.

Several states, on the other hand, have issued regulations that treat software as tangible for the purpose of imposing a sales tax on a purchase. The question is far from settled, and will continue to vary from state to state until a firm national policy is declared in a Supreme Court test case.

INVESTMENT TAX CREDIT (ITC)

The Internal Revenue Service has issued several rulings on questions about investment tax credit for both hardware and software. They have held that:

> Where a bundled computer is purchased, the cost of the computer includes the cost of the software, and the ITC is available.
>
> When a purchaser is required to make structural changes in the office; for example, the cost of raised flooring for wiring air conditioning ducts, such alterations qualify for the ITC.
>
> When a computer-controlled fire detection system, designed to remain in place permanently, is installed, it does not qualify for the ITC.

DEPRECIATION

The Reagan Administration's tax bill, which passed in 1981, changed the rulings on depreciation. Prior to the passage of that bill most business equipment, including computer equipment, has been written off over a 7–12 year period. With the Economic Recovery Tax Act of 1982, the cost of nearly all machinery and equipment will be deductible over a 5-year period.

PATENTS

Another legal issue that will be in the forefront of industry discussions during the next few years, is the question of patents on computer equipment and peripherals. During 1981, the United States Supreme Court upheld a lower court ruling that a Honeywell Information Systems computer, containing software imbedded on a chip that directs the transfer of data within the computer, is a patentable invention.

The Court's decision says that the Honeywell employees who developed this particular chip are entitled to a patent on the product. This decision, along with a series of Supreme Court decisions, permitting patents of new industrial processes that combine existing or new computer programs with other technical procedures, provides some clear direction on the handling of computer patent questions.

Until now, computer manufacturers could patent only some hardware. Now entire computer machines are considered as patentable inventions.

COPYRIGHT

As indicated in Chapter Six, the question of software copyright is far less settled than is the question of patents. Recent rulings have not provided the kind of guidelines needed to clarify this issue, and the question will be addressed over and over again in the courts until a clear cut definition is available. Basically, printed descriptions of the computer machines and circuits, programs, program listings, technical drawings, manuals, advertisements, and catalogs, are all copyrightable as literary or pictorial works. Not protected by copyright are the ideas, systems, processes, concepts, or discoveries of the hardware described or illustrated in the work. There is no copyright protection available for the machine hardware itself. The copyright protection on software is very hazy at this point, providing protection only in very specific instances.

Collections of data, such as printed directories and statistical indexes and summaries, have been protected by copyrights. Also protected are "computer programs in general." According to a decision in May 1964, of the Registry of Copyrights, a program is copyrightable regardless of the form in which it was created—whether as a flow chart, as a listing, or as a deck of machine readable cards, as on a disc or other memory element. However, if the program is in bubble memory or in a delay line, the law is not clear. Some still argue, on constitutional grounds, that programs are not copyrightable. The question is yet to be resolved. (*Computers & The Law, An Introductory Handbook,* Commerce Clearing House Inc., Third Edition, 1981.)

COMPUTER SECURITY

Other legal issues that computer users have to personally consider pertain to the security of their own computer systems and the files contained therein. A bank official of the Wells Fargo Co. was charged with a $21.3 million computer fraud. This one computer heist netted more than half the total take of all U.S. bank robberies during 1980.

The spread of computer fraud is due to the spread of computer technology and the increasing use of central computers the files of which can be entered via a telephone connection, using a personal computer terminal. The trend of the industry to provide easy-to-use systems has made the technology accessible to virtually the entire literate population of the world. Personal computers potentially could tap into data transmissions, either to steal proprietary information or to insert fraudulent messages that could, for example, transfer money from one bank account to another. In one instance, a 15-year-old boy in Berkeley, California, operating a terminal from his home, managed to connect to the main computer at the campus of the University of California, Berkeley and destroy valuable research files.

Although sophisticated software programs are available, which are designed to restrict access to computer files, they are not "fail safe." Nor are they always used by companies who might need them. White collar computer crime is creating opportunities that have never before been available for those who wish to cheat. For example, a clerk in the Motor Vehicles Department in New York was caught changing computer records so that car thieves were listed as the owners of the stolen vehicles. In this instance, as in many others, the office managers failed to address the need for sophisticated anti-fraud measures.

Computer security, at too many companies, has merely meant that computer rooms have had private guards standing outside, or elaborate locks on the doors, and magnetic card access systems with entry limited to only a select few.

With distributed processing and office automation bringing computers out of computer rooms and to the offices and desks of all employees, physical security alone is nearly impossible and certainly impractical.

Newly developed sophisticated computer security products and services are available. These include software to restrict computer access and to simplify computer audits; hardware to scramble computer transmissions that might go out over telecommunications facilities, and various systems designed to assist the computer itself in detecting and reporting attempted fraud.

In addition, specific safeguard measures can be undertaken to prevent computer fraud. They include:

1. Physical security—the use of effective locks, bolts, and data center access controls to prevent break-ins and entry by unauthorized individuals.
2. A close look at employment hiring practices in screening individuals who will be involved in computer functions—both in data processing and in information processing—realizing that when an employee is terminated he might be more inclined to take revenge on the computer files.
3. Appropriate controls on applications systems and documentation, including the use of passwords to enter and leave the system, and a way to change the password at frequent intervals so that they cannot be "leaked" out to unauthorized individuals.
4. Careful monitoring of sensitive and proprietary files, and a separate set of passwords for these files.
5. The implementation of a computer audit at frequent enough intervals to insure the continuance of appropriate security controls over the system.

A computer audit is an independent and objective review of the information system and its use, including records, activities, and organizational responsibilities. The audit covers three areas: a broad-based review of the system design to determine the adequacy of controls; a software audit designed to assure software quality; a monitoring surveillance that analyzes and evaluates the possibility of weaknesses and problems in the system. The audit is an expensive and intricate procedure and certainly, for the small business, would be a difficult expenditure to cost-justify.

As with all else in the computer field, security concerns are just beginning to surface. They will be addressed in a variety of ways in the office of the future; from one experiment, which would verify authorized terminal users by electronically analyzing their signatures, to systems that will be able to recognize human voice and determine a user's clearance.

With new light sensitive silicon chips being developed, perhaps computers will automatically take a picture of a person and search for a clearance retained in its memory, before he/she is allowed to access the stored files.

As with other legal issues, questions of computer security are far from settled and will continue to plague computer users until a fool-proof method is found.

TELECOMMUNICATIONS ??

Another area which has not been clearly defined through legislation is the question of the communications of computer output from one party to another. We are currently living under the restrictions and regulations of the Communications Act of 1938—written long before "high tech" was a part of the vocabulary. The Act is in the throes of being rewritten in order to address the concerns and needs of a growing telecommunications industry.

The proliferation of networks and the expansion of satellite services, as well as the question of who will provide telecommunications services and how those services will be provided, are complex issues that will take many years to straighten out.

For the individual purchasing a small standalone system, this issue is certainly not of major concern. However, for the business that plans to expand its computing use to include not only the processing, storage, and retrieval of information, but the communication of that information to a location outside the perimeters of a particular building in which the computer is sitting, the final decisions regarding telecommunications bear watching.

For telecommunications users in the United States, the impact of the Bell System's role, and decisions as to who the common carriers will be, and who will provide private networks, are important questions to be answered.

Other issues in the telecommunications arena involve the security of transmissions and the issuance of common protocol standards, so that there is some degree of compatibility with equipment when networks begin to fill.

Legal issues, as they relate to the computer industry, are so complex that, in the future, a whole new body of law will be written to answer some of the concerns and alleviate some of the disagreements that arise. They are concerns that will affect all computer users.

Chapter Nine

Training

After you are sure all the agonies and ecstasies of adding a computer system to your office have been experienced and the system is installed, the most traumatic realization—how do you operate this system???—comes next. A lag exists between the capabilities of information processing equipment when it is brought into an office and the use of the system. People don't learn to use these computers overnight. Studies have shown that information processing tools are generally used inefficiently; and that it takes users a long time to realize that the machinery can perform several functions. In many offices, people are using only 10 percent of the capabilities of their small computers and word processing terminals.

As indicated in previous chapters, when a buyer reviews the contract to purchase a computer, it is important to be clear on the type of training and support that is offered with the system at no charge, and what training is available, even if a fee is required.

It is estimated that by 1990 more than 20 percent of the U.S. Labor force will require some knowledge of automated information processing. General office workers, with increasing access to workstations and databases, will need new skills to perform their jobs. In addition, office managers and executives need to understand the concepts and parameters of their own system in relation to its impact on the organization.

How are these "computer skills" going to be absorbed by a workforce that barely has time to complete the day-by-day tasks? Clearly, there is a generation gap of people to whom the computer is a foreign object, as opposed to the next generation of workers who, as youngsters, are being exposed now to computer workstations from the time they enter elementary school. They will be computer literate and as comfortable with the workstation as the current working population is with the telephone.

Although a number of computer courses are being offered by various educational institutions as a part of both degree-granting programs and as continuing education courses, this pathway to a computer literate population is slow, painful, and inadequate to meet the growing need.

The American Electronic Association projected in 1981 that the electronic industry alone could hire nearly 200,000 electronics graduates through 1985 and that, given current enrollments, only a third, or about 70,000, would be available. The U.S. Department of Labor, Bureau of Labor Statistics, also issued a projection that shows the demand for mechanics to service data processing equipment will nearly triple by 1990, to as many as 172,000.

High tech. experts estimate that more than 60 million workers from the total American work force of approximately 110 million workers will be using a workstation by 1990. The annual production of workstations is expected to surpass 5 million units annually by 1990.

Numbers aside, when your office buys a computer system, someone had better understand how to operate it!

When computers for the office first came on the market, they were generally sold with week-long workshops, taught by experts, and attended by several individuals from an office who wanted to learn how to operate the system. This was a part of the package provided with the purchase. Vendors also made available field technicians, who would be at the new user's office for many hours from the time the system arrived, to help out with any snags. This procedure became very costly to the vendors who were selling more and more systems and, suddenly, could not keep up with the demands of all their new clients.

A newer approach to support services has resulted that includes the installation to telephone hotlines, available on a 24 hour basis, to answer user questions and save the technician for the more difficult and unusual situations.

Along with the hotlines, the new users are given self-paced training packets to teach them the basics of how to operate the system. These self-paced training packets usually consist of audio-cassettes, manuals, and guidebooks. The cassettes and manuals are usually modular and provide step-by-step instruction, which on many terminals, is also reiterated on the screen through menus that are provided.

Some of the disadvantages of this approach to training is that it is tedious and cumbersome. The manuals tend to be too complicated and often do not present material in a logical sequence. There is often an inconsistency of terms that makes looking up a specific procedure or function difficult. The amount of text material is overwhelming and the pace of the audio-cassettes is slow and simplistic, making them intolerable for managers and executives, who generally do not have the patience for all this. As time passes, vendors will gain experience with the self-paced training packets and will improve their presentation and format.

While these developments in training have unfolded, a parallel development in computer design has also taken place that has made systems more "user friendly," or easy to use. Vendors have spent a great deal of time and money in the late 1970s and early 1980s designing systems that contain more memory and cheaper processing power, which includes "menus," "help" keys, and other ease-of-use features that decrease the need for formal training. Eventually it is projected that no training will be necessary to operate a computer. A user will simply sit down at the terminal, activate the on/off switch and be able to begin working.

This premise, however, does not help today's new buyer utilize a new computer system to its capacity. While deciding on which system to buy, the provision of adequate training must be kept in mind if the ultimate goals of the organization are to be achieved.

Several factors must be remembered. First, the buyer must consider the reputation of the vendor who is to support the system. It is important to be sure that the vendor from whom you are buying is well established, financially sound, and will be able to support the system for both training and repair problems. As new software is developed for the system it is important that you are provided with adequate materials (called documentation), to enable you to use that software.

Most reputable vendors offer some free basic training on their equipment, even if it is a half-morning for one employee. All established vendors have additional courses at satellite training centers, which users can attend for a fee. Some vendors also offer on-site training to users and they provide the instructors and materials for a per-hour fee. Certain vendors also offer a series of monthly seminars for an annual charge, and reduced rates if several employees wish to attend. It is important for the buyer to check, in advance, the course offerings of his supplier to see if they adequately meet his needs.

In larger corporations, management training, which has always been a corporate responsibility, must take on the added function of providing courses from which the company will ultimately gain a skilled computer literate labor force. This means there must be in-house courses for all levels of management. Secretaries, managers, and executives need to be given the opportunity to learn how to operate the company's computer systems. Courses must also be available that address the needs of the new organizational structure, which encompasses the dynamics of automating the office.

In smaller organizations that cannot afford to establish in-house training programs, there will continue to be a glut of seminars and workshops that address the issues of office automation. Managers must give careful consideration to which courses are beneficial. They are all costly. Be sure that the courses your employees attend are being given by reputable advisory groups, such as the American Management Association and such other established learning centers as large universities or government institutions. There is much misinformation being passed around in this field.

Training is also available through audio-visual libraries that incorporate videotaped lectures and video discs. Usually an organization will contract with a supplier of these libraries for a series of audio-visual lecture courses to be provided over a one-year period. Suppliers of these services include: Edutronics of Overland Park, Kansas, owned by McGraw Hill; Deltrak, Incorporated of Oak Brook, Illinois, owned by Prentice-Hall; and Advanced Systems Inc. of Elk Grove, Illinois. The videotapes range in subject matter from direct instruction in word processing technique to management strategies.

Other training avenues that will be in evidence more and more in the next decade include: the use of video discs to provide managers and executives with updates on technology; on sociological and behavioral changes that affect the work environment; and video teleconferencing from vendor to user, with a trainer who will provide advice remotely rather than via the personal office visit.

As computer systems become easier to use and the number of employees who are familiar with computers expands, less training will be needed. Meanwhile the wise buyer had better map out a training strategy before signing on the dotted line.

Chapter Ten

Databases

The hardware has been evaluated...ordered...installed. The software is in place. You have attended your orientation sessions, and the vendor's sales representative and training people have explained the system, and have helped you learn how to operate it. Your initial apprehensions are gone....

This is the time when the value of your system will either be realized or will be forfeited. It is the time to form your permanent database the backbone of your information processing, and the rationale for justifying the purchase that you probably have not yet paid for.

A database is a collection of data that is shared and used for multiple purposes by many individuals. It is the foundation of your system upon which many layers of growth will occur, and many levels of capabilities will ensue. Inputting the appropriate information files to form a database for your new computer system is the most important task you will face. It is the most difficult as well.

Hopefully, when you thought about putting in a computer system you conducted an information study to determine just what it is that you process every day, each week, and during the month. This study now becomes an important part of the integration of the system into your office environment, as you look at the material that needs to be logged into the computer step-by-step.

No amount of fancy hardware and sophisticated software will provide you with a ready-made database suited to meet your individual needs. The reasons for a database are to:

1. Centralize your data so that it can be accessible to many individuals as a basic resource.
2. Make data as useful as possible to all the individuals in an organization, including the decision makers.
3. Permit constant modification of data.
4. Allow for a "search" to obtain answers to queries or information for planning purposes.
5. Provide a way of getting data to several locations through telecommunications links (usually in larger companies that are spread over several locations).

On the basis of these reasons, you must now decide what information is going into the database and how that information must be organized, so that you will have dynamic, flexible files that will endure your demands, and yet be adaptable to change when new applications need to be added.

The first step is to determine what must go into the computer, and in what order. What is the most important file of material that is needed on the computer? This could be copies of repetitive forms that your secretaries are constantly retyping. It may be a listing of all your clients or customers, with a descriptive phrase or sentence about each one. It may be a list of all outstanding bills, or a list of all incoming receipts. Whatever you decide, you must prepare a master list of the informational units that you wish to input one at a time onto a disk. When one disk is completely filled you go on to another disk, logging on a master disk as well as in a paper file just what is being stored where. Remember, when creating a database, organization is the key.

Once the first set of materials has been input, another batch of information follows. You have to determine if there are any lists that will need to be processed. You will have to search through your files for key paragraphs that recur in your reports, proposals, and memorandum. You have to input the copy contained in letters, speeches, annual reports, and other documents that appear with frequent regularity.

An individual who is creating a database may find that he/she is developing a series of abbreviations, or a system of shorthand to denote certain repetitive terms or phrases that keep reappearing. This "coded" information has to be filed in a printed glossary, so that other users of the system will understand just what those terms mean. Some systems come with a glossary capability that enables the user to automatically generate and file a listing of "user signals." If a glossary capability is not one of the features on your system, you will need to devise a system for retaining and communicating the coded terminology to all users of the system.

Often in companies that have had little or no experience in data processing, different individuals will develop different names for the same data item, and sometimes the same names for different data items. For computers to work well for everyone, uniformity and precision is needed when a database is formed. It is up to the user who is initially creating the database to make sure that the appropriate data is correctly designed, and appropriately organized, and protected.

Only with the proper structure of the database will computer users in an office be able to realize the full potential of the stored data. As the need for information increases, the ability of the computer to deal with requests for that information will become more and more dependent upon how the database was organized at the time the system was installed. Provide the organized structure for future expansion and growth, and the database will provide you with a smooth and efficient system.

A database can consist of text, numbers, graphics, or a combination of all three. It is obvious that forming the database takes a great deal of planning. In summary, consider the following questions:

1. Who needs to access this database?
2. What information do they need?
3. How are they going to use that information?
4. How is the information going to be disseminated?
5. Do I understand my equipment well enough to go ahead and plan out my database?
6. All of the above considered, what will I put into the computer and in what order?
7. Am I going to use a language of codes and shorthand signals for myself, and how do I formulate a glossary, so that others will understand my signals?

DATABASE MANAGEMENT SYSTEMS (DBMS)

Several companies offer software packages that organize, enhance, and control the applications software of a system, so that a single collection of information can be processed in different ways for different purposes. These are called Database Management Systems (DBMS). The programs of a DBMS retrieve and manipulate data contained on a regular computer system. They help to structure the database and provide access to it through a network. Essentially designed for environments of medium and larger companies, which may have several locations, these systems enable the user to organize their electronic files and generate the most effective use possible of information in the system.

The DBMS is an entity that provides programmers and end users with the data they request. Working independently from the actual applications programs, the DBMS organizes, controls, and retrieves information and provides the end user with easy access.

The major advantage to this sophisticated software is that it organizes a corporation's data in line with the way the company uses it, making it easier for unskilled computer users. A database management system also cuts programming time because data once entered works in many programs.

EXTERNAL DATABASE RESOURCES

The computer user should be aware that there are hundreds of external databases, which he can log on to, that provide immediate access to information on every imaginable subject. The world at large is going "online" and, during the 1980s, revenues to suppliers and distributors of online database services is expected to soar past the $1.5 billion dollar mark each year of the decade. Professionals in every field can find instant information processed, stored, and delivered electronically at the mere touch of a button.

Attorneys can now search and locate citations and histories on every case from a lower court decision to a U.S. Supreme Court mandate, by subscribing to one of the several legal databases now available.

In the medical field there are databases that provide information on the most recent discoveries in cancer, blood, and heart research. An online biomedical database is available for a literature search regarding current biomedical research; and information on the latest scientific, chemical, and engineering discoveries is accessible to those who need it.

The New York Times Information Service has established a database that provides current information on economic, financial, and political development in the Middle East. Various economic databases are available to tell the user everything from up-to-the-minute stock market quotations, to forecasting projections on the demand for petroleum products in a specific region of the world.

There are databases to help individuals choose a college by merely plugging in the factors desired in a college and asking for a print out of the schools that meet the criteria. There are also databases to help an employee who has been transferred find an apartment, by requesting a list of all available properties in a particular area.

Business and financial data on various companies has been compiled into a database developed from annual reports and quarterly statements, and business statistics on companies doing business in over 130 countries is now available online.

One condominium developer in New York City offers its residents an online database, containing 1,200 information and communication services, including financial quotation news and travel schedules. Another database service provides a detailed analysis of how various congressmen and senators voted on issues, and a break down of the advocates and adversaries by a particular issue or bill being discussed.

Databases are also available within large organizations that provide employees, who may be located all over the world, information on such miscellaneous items as how a local football team is doing, or what the weather is in London on a certain day.

Whole libraries are being put on computers and the information is becoming available to the public. The terminals to get into these databases are usually located at a local library branch, and can be used by everyone desiring to tap in.

Databases have answered the information explosion problem with the fast and easy access they provide to information requests. Will the result be a better informed, more capable cadre of decision makers?

PART THREE

COMMUNICATING IN THE OFFICE OF THE FUTURE

We are standing today on the threshold of a new technology that brings voice, print, data video, and other media into a comprehensive, fully integrated office information system. This is a period when the nuts and bolts of computer use are being formulated. Hardware is becoming less expensive; software is becoming easier; printers are improving in quality, speed, and size.

During the coming decade, intelligent hardware will become common and will perform the majority of repetitive, mundane office functions without an operator's assistance. A common computer language will be designed for ready access by untrained personnel. Step-by-step integration of each function in the office will take place and the office will become a node for an integrated communication system.

The office of the future will be a place where the secretaries' role will no longer be; and in his/her place will be an administrative assistant, who will find that repetitive chores are completed by a computer and the more interesting functions of dealing with other people and directing the flow of information will be an increasing larger part of the daily routine.

It will be a place where executives will make decisions with the aid of computer terminals, which will provide not only basic information quickly and easily, but which will also provide a computer's diagnosis of problems, as well as the various solutions. Those same executives will be able to do much of their work in the den of their home, using sophisticated communicating computers that keep in touch with the office or laboratory through intricate communication pathways, which will be in place.

Automatic speech recognition will become a realistic alternative to the use of keyboards, enabling people to talk to computers that will respond to those oral commands and requests. Chips that can see will bring forth optical computers that deal with video images, rather than strings of digital codes. Supercomputers, up to 100 times faster than the most powerful models available in the 1980s, will continue to dazzle the market as will the capabilities of chips that, by 1990, are estimated to hold not the 65,000 bytes of data that a single chip can currently hold, but an incredible 1 million bytes!

The substitution of microform for paper in records storage will become an increasingly attractive, and legally acceptable way to save large amounts of space, and provide quick and easy access to various pieces of information. Already the technology has provided the ability to record computer output directly into microforms, rather than printing it out. Computer output to microform (COM) will save companies thousands of dollars in space and personnel, as computer terminals proliferate in the office.

Some futurists even predict that the office of the future will include artificial intelligent machines that will be able to explore significant mathematical, scientific, or engineering alternatives, at a rate far exceeding the human ability. These robots, in the world of tomorrow, will perform many functions, including the diagnosis of what is wrong with the very computers that created them.

The Office of the Future—it has already started with the placement of vast networks of communication facilities that provide the channels for such office "systems" as electronic mail. It will become more apparent as the elimination of paper becomes a fact, and not a wild scheme of a dreamer. It will become a reality as the science of robotics comes to the office. In some areas it will be paperless. The office of the future—it is the challenge of the future.

Chapter Eleven

Electronic Mail

With information processing firmly implanted in the office, electronic mail follows. Business communication studies show that over 85 percent of all business communication is carried on by means of the written word. This includes the thousands of letters, memoranda and reports that are written every day.

The U.S. Post Office reported that of the $16.4 billion in revenue it collected in 1980, 84 percent was due to business mail.

Paperwork costs billions of dollars to generate, process, and store and has become a great burden to business. Electronic mail is one of the ways to cope with this problem.

In the strictest sense, electronic mail is merely an "electronic" transmission of those communications that need to be sent from location "A" to location "B." It is a system to facilitate the transfer of information. With the proper implementation, electronic mail promises not only to be a transmission agent, but also a way to alter the volume and the nature of the information currently being sent.

In other words, electronic mail systems should provide business with a solution to the paperwork burden by providing, not only a faster means of transmitting information, but a new format for sending fewer messages and a way to efficiently store those messages.

A by-product of electronic mail is the realization by offices that information management is a necessary part of running the business efficiently. A closer look at the type and format for messages being sent will, hopefully, result in more efficient information processing in the future, with fewer messages processed to fewer individuals.

The concept of electronic mail is not new. Over 100 years ago the telegraph was invented. This is a device that uses electrical impulses over a communications facility to send information from one terminal to another, and is a most primitive form of electronic mail.

For several decades now the "TWX/Telex," expanding upon the principles of the telegraph, has been used to transmit information. There are also private line teletypes, and specialized direct dial networks that have been sending information from one location to another for many years. They, too, are essentially forms of electronic mail, offering direct transmission from party A to party B at high speeds and with a degree of efficiency.

The expansion of electronic mail systems is dependent upon the placement of channels for the distribution of these communications. Current telecommunication technology is merging telephones, computers, television, and other media into communications systems capable of transmitting both voice and data among people and between machines. For a long time, voice and computer data has been transmitted over the existing telephone system. Although this has worked, it has proven to be a painfully slow and costly way for digital transmissions.

The proliferation of devices needing to talk to one another, and needing to communicate with people, has forced the establishment of networks of communications facilities to handle this demand. By 1990 it is expected that expenditures for communication facilities will be in the range of $60 billion annually. This marketplace will see the expansion of both local and long distance or global networks, providing the infinite number of channels needed.

Satellite communications will also speed the development of electronic mail over the next decade. The availability of the wideband transmission channels provided by the satellites will lower the cost of electronic mail and increase the facilities that are available for a larger user base.

Satellite carriers are the most economic alternative for the types of transmission that require wide bandwidth (up to several megabytes per second), such as high-speed batch transfer of computer data, or high speed digital facsimile. (An ordinary telephone channel offers a maximum bandwidth of 9,600 bytes per second.)

Besides providing the wideband channels that are needed, satellites offer many other exciting capabilities. Conventional carriers force a user to implement a network of stages. The satellite provides users with an integrated network and not simply a group of circuits. Because satellite services provide simultaneous and full interconnection among all earth stations, a user can implement an organization-wide network to carry all its messages. The flexibility available with satellites is another plus in their favor. An organization can continually reassign satellite capacity to meet its varying needs, both geographically and in terms of the mix of communication traffic. With their point-to-multipoint or broadcast capability, satellites facilitate not only electronic mail, but transmission of many other business applications.

There are many advantages to electronic mail systems. Studies show that they will alter the efficiency, productivity, and eventually the bottom line in an office. Electronic mail is person-to-person communciation using a computer. It is noninterruptive, that is, unlike the telephone call, an electronic message can be stored and reviewed when a manager has time to give it his attention. Also unlike the telephone, electronic mail is not dependent upon the constraint of locating a specific individual at a specific moment.

Although electronic mail can be used to communicate between the person receiving a message and the person sending the message, it may also involve many individuals at the same time, without the additional burden of sending "carbon" or "xerox" copies. In other words, as long as an individual has access to a terminal, he may be included in an electronic message. As a result, electronic mail is intended to replace both the multifold telephone calls made and received by most managers during the day and will, hopefully, cut down on the number of repetitive written communications that are sent out.

Electronic mail also provides a new medium for geting certain tasks within a company done more quickly and with less expense. For example, many companies regularly poll their employees on various matters. Electronic systems could be utilized for these surveys with little expenditure of time or effort.

The system could also serve as employee/suggestion/complaint services, providing a new way for employees to express their opinions without the need for a lot of written messages. Terminals, located at strategic areas of a company, could be utilized by any employee wishing to record a suggestion or complaint at set times during the week. A special code could be designated that would establish the confidentiality of the message. The messages could be stored and reviewed by the executive in charge of this project at his convenience.

Eventually, electronic mail systems will link to the executive's home, enabling him to "handle" his correspondence during periods when he has no other interruptions or pressures. Many electronic mail terminals will plug into an electrical outlet at a home or hotel room, and by patching them into the telephone system, instant retrieval of messages in an electronic mailbox is possible.

As more and more hand-held terminals come on the market, the toting of an electronic mailbox becomes almost a certainty among busy executives who travel a lot and who do not enjoy spending a day reviewing the mail after a trip. There are several approaches to electronic mail from which the user may choose.

FACSIMILE

One of the entrants in the electronic mail arena is facsimile. Facsimile units provide a hard-copy duplicate of an original, including a signature, and any drawings and graphic materials. Initial facsimile equipment was not overwhelmingly received because of its poor reproduction quality and slow transmission speed (up to six minutes per page). That is changing with newer facsimile machines capable of running at two minutes or less per page. Newer

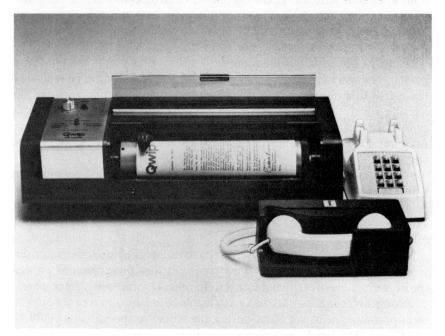

FIGURE 11-1   Exxon Quip Facsimile. Exxon Office Systems Company manufactures the portable QWIP 1200 desk facsimile unit which sends and receives pictures and letters over an ordinary telephone in 4 or 6 minutes. The added benefit of a Contrast Control allows the user to adjust the lightness and darkness of copy sent or received. Expressly designed for customers who must communicate priority mail, the QWIP 1200 is compatible with most of the facsimile machines on the market. Exxon Office Systems Company also markets the QWIP TWO, a 2 and 3 minute unit which operates worldwide and a 2, 3, 4 and 6-minute automatic unit which works by itself day or night. Facsimile increases efficiency, makes it easier to meet deadlines and saves messenger and express mail costs.
(Courtesy of Exxon Enterprises)

fax machines are also meeting internationally adopted standards, which resolve some of the incompatibility problems that formerly plagued users. Advances in facsimile technology and the availability of wideband transmission facilities will increase the usage of high speed fax units as electronic message systems.

One of the problems, however, is the fact that facsimile documents that have been received are not machine-readable and, therefore, cannot be automatically logged into the computer terminal. Newer systems include such features as high volume document feeders, improved scanners, and automatic dialing and network control functions that will aid in the automatic transfer of copy to and from remote locations.

Facsimile, used in combination with optical character readers (OCR), not only increases the speed with which a document can be sent, but also, in some cases, will eliminate a complete manual step. Using an OCR scanner, it is possible to have an operator keyboard a message one time on an electronic typewriter that uses an OCR type font, and feed it through the fax machine, which will automatically generate and send the message.

COMMUNICATING WORD PROCESSORS

Another format for electronic mail is through a network of communicating word processors. In order for a system of communicating word processors to succeed, every manager in the department or company must have a terminal that is linked to the terminals of other managers, and to a "host" computer. The ability of these terminals to "talk to one another" provides an electronic mail system that eliminates not only paper but also many redundant telephone calls received during a day.

With the infrastructure of a large company, a system of communicating word processors is often the most logical way to implement an electronic mail system. Often the terminals are tied together through the company's already existing mainframe. They communicate by telephone lines. Working out the details of time on the mainframe and the logistics of the capacity of the computer to handle the electronic messaging, although a large task, is not impossible, and the ultimate cost justification can usually be determined.

As more and more managers begin to utilize word processing for their own needs and not just as substitute typewriters for their secretaries, communicating word processing will become prolific in the office. With the advent of local networks, communications capabilities will become greatly enhanced, lowering the cost of communications and making electronic mail a reality in a number of diverse situations.

COMPUTER BASED MESSAGE SYSTEMS

Another approach to electronic mail that has been slowly developing is "Computer Based Message Systems" (CBMS), or electronic messaging. A number of private companies market these systems, where a central computer on which the user "shares" time, acts as a "traffic cop" for receiving and transmitting messages that the users prepare on a video terminal. The messages are stored in an electronic "mailbox" at the location of the recipient and can be read and answered at the recipient's convenience. This approach enables the manager to be free from the constant interruptions of telephone messaging. Because all messages are stored on disk, the manager has the security of knowing that he can save and recall what he wishes, and erase the remainder of his electronic mail. Many of the CBMS systems have text editing capability, so that the messages entered for electronic mail purposes can be edited before they are sent.

YANKEE GROUP STUDY

According to a Yankee Group survey of a population of over 600 electronic mail users, electronic mail increased productivity and decreased the number of memos, telephone calls, and meetings that executives, using a system, were attending. The results of the survey revealed the following:

	Yes	No
Increase in productivity	57%	43%
Decrease in Memos	63%	37%
Decrease in telephone use	53%	37%
Decrease in meetings	15%	85%

Other significant findings revealed that electronic mail decreased the number of telephone calls made and enabled the initiator of the mail message to reach a group of individuals in the single broadcast, and not just the one individual that a telephone call normally contacted.

The study reached the conclusion that electronic mail alters our format for doing business. The Yankee Group stated:

> The primary benefit of electronic mail is that it is a new style of communication. It is our conclusion that it is going to drastically change the way companies and people do business. The goal of electronic mail is to maximize the human element of the corporation. This productivity/performance increase

will be difficult to nail down, but it will be there. It allows more concise, more focused, less inhibited communciations. It cuts right to the heart of the problem or allows the "fuzziness" to stand out so brightly that it can be corrected. It increases the speed of communications and thus increases the speed of turnaround time. It expands the business day and allows corporations to operate more effectively over time zones and even across multi-national barriers. While electronic mail has the potential to reduce travel costs, mail costs, and document preparation costs, these savings are only minor in comparison to its primary mission: manager productivity increase." (Yankee Group Report on Electronic Mail, December 1978)

IMPLEMENTATION

Unfortunately in many companies, the planning and budgeting for electronic mail systems is being done in a disorganized fashion, and there is a proliferation of electronic mail applications to existing equipment without a precise structure in mind.

One large bank, for example, has a system for sending external messages electronically all over the world. Through its "automated wire room," the bank is able to send a message from any office in its headquarters to anyone outside that building, without human intervention, after the initial message has been keyboarded. The system took the bank two years to develop and involved an expenditure of nearly two million dollars. It is electronic mail at its best, but is not recognized as such. Within the bank's internal organization, no electronic mail system has ever been considered.

On the other hand, there are several examples where electronic mail systems are working very successfully.

At one large bank, more than a thousand employees are linked by the bank's computer mail system, which has cut paper processing by 90%, giving the managers more time to spend with their subordinates.

At a large industrial complex, more than 8,000 terminals in 18 countries are linked by the firm's computer mail network, which carries four million messages each year.

Even the U.S. Post Office is getting into the electronic mail act. The Postal Service's proposed entry into the electronic mail field involves three facets: Electronic Computer Originated Mail (ECOM), which would accept billing data directly from company computers, forward it to the nearest post office, and there convert the data into printed bills for mailing. Electronic Message Service System (EMSSO) which, in its most advanced form would enable the USPS to "carry" mail from one home computer to another without ever handling paper, and "Intelpost," which would use facsimile transmission to forward mail overseas. Intelpost would connect with similar systems available in various countries throughout the world.

Like everything else, universal acceptance of electronic mail will not be without its pains and problems. Many current electronic mail devices are not compatible with other pieces of equipment. Two different word processing devices, for example, often cannot communicate. Many pieces of equipment are not compatible with the networks that they eventually will want to link into. Furthermore, historically, electronic mail systems have evolved to handle specialized applications, with no real intention of pervading an entire company. These diverse systems often cannot communicate with one another. In the office of the future they will need to communicate, not only internally, but with the outside world as well.

The current trend toward purchase of self-contained standalone terminals will not advance the communications function either, unless they have the ability to communicate with a variety of devices and pieces of apparatus.

Electronic mail systems also tend to be viewed with suspicion by many managers who are reluctant to use terminals.

When word processing becomes accepted practice in the office, as the telephone and typewriter have been, it will become obvious that terminals, sitting idly, serve nobody. It will also become obvious that electronic mail holds great promise to alleviate the paper burden that the society has fostered for so long.

Some of the task-oriented changes that will be obvious with automation and electronic mail systems are illustrated as follows:

Manual Processing	*Electronic Processing*
Document Preparation	Text Entry / Editing
Filing	Information Retrieval
Mailing Lists	List Processing
Scheduling	Calendar / Tickler File
Copying	Intelligent Copiers / Printers
Storage	Micrographics
Drawing Visuals	Computer Graphics
Research	Database Access
Travel / Meetings	Teleconferencing
Mail	Electronic Mail
Telephone Calls	Voice Store and Forward
Printing	Photocomposition
Computation	Data Processing
Records Keeping	Records Processing

Chapter Twelve

Robotics

We are becoming the servants in thought, as in action of the machine we have created to serve us.

John Kenneth Galbraith
The New Industrial State, Ch. 1, 1967

When economist John Kenneth Galbraith made that statement in 1967, it was dubious that he was talking about artificial intelligent machines. Dramatic progress has been made during the past decade in microelectronics and technology will continue to produce smaller, more powerful, and less expensive computers, whose thinking capability is limited to that which is programmed in by man. Although we talk of "intelligent terminals" as opposed to "dumb terminals" and "intelligent printers," the word is being used to mean intelligent: as a characteristic of being programmed to follow certain directions with no thought as to what to do if the circumstances were to change.

Intelligence is more. It is that ingredient unique to higher beings that enables them to perceive the world and make sense of a number of stimuli. As far as we know, human beings have qualities that distinguish them from intelligent animals, such as dogs or monkeys, enabling them to formulate and pursue goals and to think through particular problems. In other words, human beings have the ability to reason, given any number of circumstances.

Artificial intelligence is the application of those characters of reacting to stimuli, or perceiving a set of circumstances, and of *reasoning*, to machine-like beings, which have been built with computerized components and have been programmed to carry out specific acts. These products, called "robots" are designed to gather and interpret data in order to permit automated machinery to perform a variety of relatively skilled functions.

Webster's dictionary defines a robot as "a machine that performs the mechanical functions of a human being." A totally inadequate definition today, robots go far beyond mechanical functions. Robots come in all shapes and sizes, from the androids of *Star Wars* to the drones of industry.

By applying all the most sophisticated techniques of computer systems to the construction of artificial intelligent machines, robots are now able to relate to visual stimuli, and to the sound of the human voice; they are able to walk, talk, and generally "think." Speech synthesis programs create voices for robots and image recognition gives them eyes. Because their instruction programs can be changed, they provide a diverse functionality that will make them continually useful to society. They can be randomly programmed to react to a number of stimuli and can have a local memory of any size desired.

Most robots today are being used for industrial applications. Because of their enormous capacity to handle sizable weights and to utilize multiple appendages, they are useful in such assembly line applications as welding, spray painting, assembly, or material handling. With their built-in vision systems they are used in inspection, counting, and sorting of materials as they come off the assembly line.

They are also used in dangerous work such as inspection chores and clean up of nuclear reactors, or in detecting unexploded bombs. It is predicted that as robot technology develops they will be used to explore the ocean floor, rescue fire victims, diagnose difficult cases for doctors, and will serve the blind as "seeing eye" helpers.

Because robots do not have the physical limitations of man—the need to breath oxygen, the need to stay away from toxic waste, the need to eat and sleep at specified intervals—they will perform a variety of tasks that far exceed man's ability to get them done. Robots can walk on two feet, but also can be constructed to have as many feet as a centipede. The Japanese have built a robot designed to walk like a spider; it is able to climb skillfully up and down ladders and stairs by extending and contracting its legs. Another robot, designed like a snake, is able to slither through narrow holes and passages picking its way through a maze of dangers. Yet another Japanese-built robot has been designed to help detect breast cancer. By means of 25 fingers, each equipped with sensitive gauges hooked to a computer, the robot is able to detect the presence of a lump and to draw a picture of the lump using computer graphics. This enables medical specialists to find the lump and treat it without exposing the patient to the harmful effects of x-ray.

Will robots come to the office in the future? Unquestionably, yes, although it is anyone's guess what chores they will perform. Already robots are being used as an efficient means for mail delivery. In most companies in the future, however, that role will be taken over by electronic mail. Although robots could be efficiently applied to some of the repetitive tasks handled today by filing clerks and secretaries, office automation will eradicate many of those chores.

In the foreseeable future, robots in the office could be set to the task of answering telephones, "manning" reception desks, and handling other repetitive inquiries. They certainly would be helpful in going out to bring back coffee. More importantly, robots could provide the means to improved

FIGURE 12-1   Robots at Work.

security for an office's physical plant, as well as a more secure system for entry into the office's computer system. The possibilities are great because robots provide attractive, viable alternatives to profit-oriented managers who see them as an adjunct to the human workforce.

Although they will replace workers, it is only in areas where the work has not been very desirable to begin with, such as on the assembly line and in nuclear plants. They will also create work in the propagation of their "species." And, they will compensate in areas where man is not able to go because of his physical limitations—in certain aspects of space exploration or in areas where men have not come up with a viable solution, such as in security. For managers the application of robots to the office and to many aspects of commercial enterprise is a boon—robots do not ask for raises!

Chapter Thirteen

A Paperless Society?

> The greatest task before civilization at present is to make machines what they ought to be, the slaves, instead of the masters of men.
>
> *Ellis Havelock*
> *Little Essays of Love and Virtue, Ch. 7, 1922*

The availability of local and long haul networks provides the business world with a number of exciting applications for more interactive communication between man and machine, between machine and machine, and among the various segments of the society.

Computer hookups from the office to the home are enabling thousands of people across the nation to "telecommute" to work, doing all kinds of jobs at home, from writing computer programs, to conducting laboratory experiments, to designing manufacturing equipment. They send their completed work, via computer, to the office where it is received by a computer and new directions or instructions are forwarded.

Voice-activated computers carry on conversations with would-be travelers who are making airline reservations for a business trip, taking down all the necessary information, and eliminating the need for filling out and recording a number of paper forms.

Patients, in remote locations, are able to have their test results and vital signs constantly monitored at the best medical centers in the world, via global

FIGURE 13-1   Wang Alliance System. Wang Audio Workstation provides voice messaging and dictation on the Alliance Office System. The Wang Audio Workstation integrates Alliance support functions, word processing, dictation, and voice messaging functions. Voice documents are created through the Audio Workstation, which has a unique digital-based voice editor that allows authors to dictate, review, and edit voice documents. The ergonomically designed workstation can also route Voicegram messages, through an automatic dialing function, to other Audio Workstation users. *(Courtesy of Wang Laboratories)*

communications links and using computer terminals, which keep an ongoing patient record available to the doctor at the press of a button. The need for lengthy medical charts and written orders is eliminated as the information is stored on computer tape.

In the offices of doctors, lawyers, insurance agents, retail stores, and wholesale manufacturers, computers keep records, log inventories, handle accounts receivables and payables, and communicate with thousands of other computers that are programmed to serve as a resource for information, diagnosis, and assistance. The process is slowly reducing the mounds of paper files that are needed.

One use to which computers and telecommunications is being put in the banking industry involves the way in which monetary payments are made.

ELECTRONIC FUND TRANSFER

Although most money payments today are still in the form of paper—utilizing bills, checks, credit card / billing arrangements—electronic fund transfer is gaining more and more momentum as the networking facilities become available.

Electronic fund transfer is the passage of money from one individual to another via machine "bits." No paper is exchanged. One computer merely keeps a record and passes information to another computer when a money transaction occurs.

Electronic Fund Transfer will eventually involve not only the transfer of money between banks, but transfers between computers of various businesses, and personal transfers of money done automatically when an individual shops or dines in a restaurant, or makes any type of a purchase. The ultimate idea is the elimination of paper money.

The installation of vast cable television networks throughout the country will be one avenue of communications to make all these, and many other applications, a reality. Cable networks and satellites, together, will provide the channels needed. Although there are a finite number of satellite orbits available, it will be many years before they are filled to capacity.

The proliferation of terminals in both the home and office will be another avenue to slowly reduce the paper avalanche, and provide the means to communicating without paper, in the office of the future.

Electronic mail systems will grow both within companies and between various institutions. As the century wears on, government or quasi-government postal services throughout the world will join the fray and institute electronic mail systems, bringing about further elimination of the written paper message.

TELECONFERENCING

The availability to managers of teleconferencing centers will also eliminate much of the corporate paperwork associated with so many meetings that occur. Teleconferencing is a means of communication by which two or more geographic sites can communicate, using electronically transmitted visual and audio information. The information is presented over a standard television monitor, or on a special screen attached to the wall of the teleconferencing center.

With satellite channels available, teleconferencing is able to link a company's offices throughout the world. One of the strongest incentives for its use is the promise of reduced travel, from both a budgetary and time spent viewpoint. It has been estimated that of all business meetings involving travel, over 35 percent could be effectively substituted with video conferencing. This will increase once people become accustomed to it. The combination of electronic mail and teleconferencing situations will virtually eliminate the need for many of the repetitive memoranda and reports that circulate in businesses. The teleconference enables a group of executives to virtually see, hear, and discuss every aspect of a proposal, budget, or other business plan. Follow-up can be done via facsimile transmissions, and on computer to computer connections.

Paper elimination will also come about as the result of new storage and retrieval techniques, vis-a-vis micrographics. Micrographic equipment now interface with computer terminals to store and generate information,

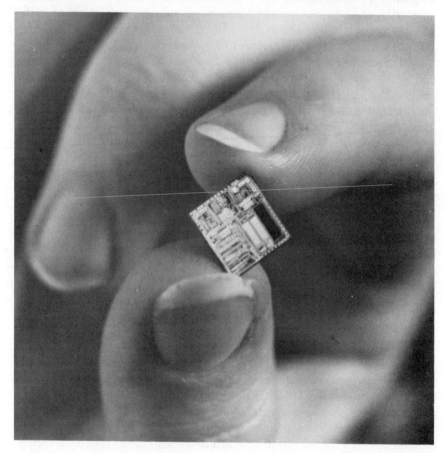

FIGURE 13–2   Digital Signal Processor Chip (AT&T). Number Cruncher—certain complicated real-time data processing tasks, previously not economically feasible, can be performed by this new Digital Signal Processor chip from Bell Labs. Able to make more than a million calculations per second, the chip may find use in applications, such as speech synthesis, voice recognition, filtering, tone detection, and line balancing in digital communications systems.
(Courtesy of AT&T)

automatically, when it is requested. Several data processing departments, in larger companies, have already completely eliminated the paper printout by connecting terminals to computer output microfilm systems (COM). COM is said to have a four-to-one cost advantage and a 100-to-one space advantage over magnetic tape. COM systems can replace up to 250 filing cabinets with a single modular terminal that can hold over one million pages of material in microfilm cartridges.

Given these statistics, it is not easy to argue against the eventual use of micrographics throughout industry—not just in libraries where micrographics first became popular. Sophisticated functions, such as adding and erasing images already on film, can now be done with micrographics. This technology is at its infancy and greater developments are sure to follow.

Will society ever totally eradicate paper? It is doubtful. In isolated situations, offices have already experimented with an operations policy of using only computer to computer messaging and communication, with no paper printout even available. However, what it receives from the outside continues to be in the form of paper and will continue in that mode for a long time to come. Isolated experiments are certainly succeeding, but in the world community it would be virtually impossible to eliminate paper from usage in the foreseeable future.

By applying the best of computer technology, however, offices will be able to better manage their resources, and more effectively control their productivity output by individuals on all levels of the office operations work force.

In the 1940s British novelist George Orwell wrote about 1984 that the world would consist of a group of people who were programmed and instructed to perform a number of functions within a rigid and specific environment. Orwell painted a picture of a society controlled via television communications, with a screen in every home, on every street corner, and in every office. Instructions to the masses of people came over this screen constantly, and the mode was to obey the instructions or die. The technology that Orwell described included two-way communication over the television monitors and pneumatic tubes that served as conveyors for information disbursal. Although the word "computer" was never once mentioned in the book, the elements of electronic technology and computers were certainly implied in the author's description of the work to come.

The technology that Orwell envisioned has now become reality, although there is no evidence that the "big brother" society he portrayed will be here in 1984. Some fear, however, that with the proliferation of computers and the increasing sophistication of robotics, elements of Orwell's *1984* are liable to befall the human race in the next century. This is the challenge of tomorrow—the challenge of how to channel the forces of the vast technology that we have built. It is, perhaps, the greatest challenge that mankind has ever sustained.

PART FOUR

APPENDIX

APPENDIX

Bibliography

Author's Note: The research for this book took more than two years and encompassed many sources, including live interviews with many vendor companies, interviews with many user companies, a survey of books written in this field, the use of industry consulting group reports, and continuous surveillance of the numerous publications that address high technology questions. Listed below are the names of vendor companies that most directly impact on the office automation market, which this book is addressing; a list of consulting groups that issue newsletters and reports; a list of some of the books now available in this field, and a comprehensive list of publications with a comment about the contents of each.

VENDOR COMPANIES IN OFFICE AUTOMATION

A. B. Dick
AM Jacquard
Apple Computer
Basic Four
Burroughs/Redactron Corporation
Cado
Canon
Casio
Compucorp
CPT Corporation

Data General
Datapoint Corporation
Digital Equipment Corporation
Exxon Information Systems
Four Phase Systems
Hazeltine Corporation
Hewlett Packard
Hitachi
Honeywell Informations Systems
International Business Machines

Lanier Business Products
Lexitron Corporation
Matsusshita
Micom Data Systems
Microdata
Mitsubishi
NBI Inc.
NCR
NEC Information Systems Inc.
Nixdorf Computer Corporation
Olivetti Corporation of America

Prime Computer
Quantel
Royal Business Machines
Shasta General Systems
Syntrex
Tandy Products
Toshiba Electric
Univac
Wang Laboratories
Wordplex
Xerox

CONSULTING GROUPS IN COMPUTER TECHNOLOGY

These groups are nationally recognized as consulting companies in new technology. They might issue periodic reports, newsletters, conduct seminars, or offer specific advice on specific projects.

Advanced Computer Techniques
Arthur D. Little
Auerbach Publishers Inc.
Booz Allen & Hamilton
Brandon Consulting Group
Chilton Research
Computer Intelligence
CRC Systems
Creative Strategies
Cuadra Associates Inc.
Datapro Research Corporation
Dataquest
Diebold Group
Faim Technical
Frost & Sullivan
Gideon Gartner Group
Gnostic Concepts
Input

International Data Corporation
International Resource Development
Kappa Group
Kessler Marketing Intelligence
Kline & Co.
Marketing Research
Martin Simpson
McKinsey & Co.
Office Technology Research Group
Oppenheimer
Predicasts
Quantum Sciences
SBS Publishing
Seybold Publications Inc.
SRI International
Venture Development Corp.
Woodward & Schaefer Inc.
Yankee Group

BOOKS

Computer Science Resources: A Guide to Professional Literature (New York: American Society for Information Science, 1981). (Note: This directory, which costs $59.50, contains more than 1,500 sources of computing information and computer-related publications.)

BIGELOW, ROBERT P., Editor, *Computers and the Law* (Chicago: Commerce Clearing House Inc., 1981).

GRAHAM, NEILL, *The Mind Tool: Computers and Their Impact on Society* (New York: West Publishing Company, 1980).

ORWELL, GEORGE, *1984* (New York: Signet, Harcourt Brace & Company Inc., 1949).
ROSEN, ARNOLD, FIELDEN, ROSEMARY, *Word Processing* (Englewood Cliffs, N.J.: Prentice-Hall, Inc., 1982).
SANDERS, NORMAN, *A Manager's Guide to Profitable Computers* (New York: American Management Association, 1978).
STEHLING, KURT R., *Computers and You* (New York: Mentor Books, 1972).
STULTZ, RUSSELL ALLEN, *The Word Processing Handbook* (Englewood Cliffs, N.J.: Prentice-Hall, Inc., 1982).
WINKLESS, NELS, BROWNING, IBEN, *Robots on Your Doorstep* (Portland, Oregon: Robotics Press, 1978).
UHLIG, RONALD, *The Office of the Future* (New York, Amsterdam: North Holland Publishing Company, 1979).
WEBSTER, TONY, *Microcomputer Buyer's Guide* (Los Angeles, CA., 1981).

PUBLICATIONS

The following publications are sources that were consulted in the research for this book. A brief description of each publication is included, so that the reader will know whether or not it is an appropriate one for consideration.

Administrative Management: Geyser-McAllister Publications Inc., 51 Madison Avenue, New York, NY 10010. A magazine containing comprehensive feature articles on office automation, and practical advice for office managers on the many questions and issues that arise when implementing office systems.
Business Communications Review: BCR Enterprises Inc., 950 York Road, Hinsdale, ILL 60521. Looks at issues in telecommunications and advances in the technology. Articles are in depth and include both features and editorials.
Byte: "The Small Systems Journal": Byte Publications Inc., 70 Main Street, Peterborough, NH 03458. A technical publication, presenting computer system specifications and information of interest to computer specialists and engineers.
Canadian Data Systems: Maclean Hunter Lmtd., 481 University Avenue, Toronto, Canada M5W1/A. Published monthly. A general interest magazine for the public at large, or members of an office environment.
Canadian Office: Whitsed Publishing Lmtd., 55 Bloor Street West, Suite 1201, Toronto, Ontario M4W3M1. A general interest publication with a focus on the office environment.
Communications News: Harcourt Brace Janovich, Geneva, ILL 60134. Published monthly. Covers total communications industry with short, easy-to-read stories, focusing on voice, video, telecommunications, and data communications. Annual subscription $16.00.
Computer Data: "Magazine for Information Management," Whitsed Publishing Lmtd., 55 Bloor Street West, Suite 1201, Toronto, Ontario M4W3M1. A general interest magazine for computer users, dealing with new equipment, issues, new developments, and trends in the industry. Essex Street, Rochelle Park, NJ 07662. Aimed at data processing managers, and includes a bit of everything. Annual subscription $26.00.
Computer Products: A synopsis of what is new in peripheral products.

Computerworld: CW Publications Inc., Box 880, 375 Cochituate Avenue, Framingham, MA 01701. A comprehensive weekly newspaper, covering all aspects of the computer community.

Computing: VNU Business Publications, 55 Frith Street, London W1A2HG. A British weekly newspaper, covering general issues that affect the computer world.

Corporate Design: 850 Third Avenue, New York, NY 10022. A magazine for facility management and planning—office design.

Corporate Systems (for Systems Managers): United Technical Publications Inc., 645 Stewart Avenue, Garden City, NY 11530. Includes general feature articles.

Creative Computing: P.O. Box 789-M, Morristown, NJ 07960. An applications and software monthly for software "literate" people who want to read about various programs.

Data Communications: McGraw Hill, Inc., 1221 Avenue of the Americas, New York, NY 10020. A monthly publication, with subscriptions limited to persons with an active professional, functional, or managerial responsibility in data communications. Somewhat technical in content.

MD Data Management: Magazine of the Data Processing Management Association, 505 Busse Highway, Park Ridge, ILL 60068.

Datamation: Monthly, Technical Publishing Company of Dun & Bradstreet Corp., 1301 South Grove Avenue, Barrington, ILL 60070. Comprehensive, in depth articles about the high tech industry.

Digital Digest: Published at 1050 Commonwealth Avenue, Boston, MA 02215. Circulation limited to only those persons who qualify in the research, development, and design engineering fields.

Electronic Business: Monthly by Cahners Publications, 221 Columbus Avenue, Boston, MA. Covers business management trends in the electronics industry, covering the gamut from data processing to office automation.

Electronic News: Fairchild Publications, 7 E. 12 Street, New York, NY 10003. General interest and technical articles aimed at persons engaged in the electronics industry.

Electronic Products: Hearst Business Communications Inc., UTP Garden City, NY 11530. A product-oriented publication for a technical person, with one or two good in-depth articles in each issue.

Electronics: Bimonthly publication of McGraw Hill Inc., 1221 Avenue of the Americas, New York, NY 02215. A highly technical publication for professionals in electronic technology. Comprehensive and well-presented.

Electronics Test: Morgan Grampian Publishing Co., 1050 Commonwealth Avenue, Boston, MA. Another highly technical publication for electronic engineers and other professionals.

Forbes: Forbes Inc., 60 Fifth Avenue, New York, NY 10011. $33.00 annual subscription. General business magazine with an occasional article on high tech.

Fortune: Biweekly by TIME Inc., 3435 Wilshire Blvd., Los Angeles, CA 90010. A feature magazine for the business community that averages at least one good high tech feature article per issue.

Harvard Business Review: Published by the Harvard Business School, Cambridge, MA. A bimonthly journal for professional managers.

High Technology: Bimonthly Technology Publishing Company, 38 Commercial Wharf, Boston, MA 02110. Feature articles on a wide range of high tech issues; written for the general public.

ICP Interface: A data processing management quarterly, published by International Computer Programming Inc., 9000 Keystone Crossing, Indianapolis, IN 46240.

IEEE Spectrum: Published monthly by the IEEE organization, 345 East 47th Street,

New York, NY 10017. A technical publication aimed at the IEEE members at a manager's position.

INC.: Monthly Inc. Publishng Co., 38 Commercial Wharf, Boston, MA 02110. General interest articles for the small business community.

Industrial Marketing: Crain Communications Inc., 740 Rush Street, Chicago, ILL 60611. General interest features for marketing managers.

Industry Week: Penton Plaza, Cleveland, OH 44138. A management magazine that covers management issues.

Information & Records Management: Monthly, 101 Crossways Park, West Woodbury, NY 11797. $10.00. Interesting and informative articles for the administrative assistant or manager involved in records management.

Infosystems: A magazine for managers concerned with office automation, containing good general feature articles on computer technology.

Infoworld: 530 Lytton, Palo Alto, CA 94301. A newsweekly publication for microcomputer users, containing news and features of general interest along with announcements of new products and other computer news.

Information Systems News: A weekly publication for MIS managers from CMP Publications Inc., 333 East Shore Road, Manhasset, NY. Circulated free to qualified management or professional personnel involved in information systems industry. Covers the general gamut of all issues and news items.

Interface Age: Computing for Business & Home. Monthly by McPheters Wolfe & Jones, 16704 Marquardt Avenue, Cerritos, CA 90701. Touches on applications of computer systems in every field, at a level for the general public.

Journal of Systems Management: Published monthly by the Association for Systems Management, 24507 Bagley Road, Cleveland, OH 44138.

Journal of Micrographics: National Micrographics Assn., 8719 Colesville Road, Silver Spring, MD 20910.

Microwave Journal: Horizon House, Ann Arbor, MI 48106. Strictly for persons concerned with VHF frequency—highly technical.

Mini Micro Systems: Cahners Publishing Co., 22 Columbus Avenue, Boston, MA 02116. Written for corporate and technical management systems engineers, with comprehensive articles on a wide variety of subjects.

MIS Week: A weekly newspaper for information management specialists, published by Fairchild Publications, 7 E. 12th Street, New York, NY 10003.

Modern Office Procedures: Penton IPC Inc., P.O. Box 95795, Cleveland, OH 44107. Monthly report on manufacturers and products.

Office Products News: Hearst Business Communications Inc., 645 Stewart Avenue, Garden City, NY 11530. Monthly update to executives in business offices on current products and related issues.

On Computing: Published four times a year. 70 Main Street, Peterborough, NH 03458. Articles of a general interest to the home computer user who wants a little technical information on software programs and on hardware.

On Line: Online Inc., 11 Tawney Land, West, CT 06883. References various database services and would be of use to managers of large computer user companies who need to be aware of these database services.

Popular Computing: Byte Publications, 70 Main Street, Peterborough, NH 03458. For home computer buffs who want to learn more about programming and various systems that are available.

Small Business Computers: 33 Watchung Plaza, Montclair, NJ 07042. Covers applications, guidelines, and product evaluations of value to users of small business computers.

Small Systems World: 950 Lee Street, Des Plaines, ILL 60016. Articles focus on specific issues for managers of departments where small business computer systems are in use.

Technology Review: Published by the Massachusetts Institute of Technology in Cambridge, MA. Feature articles of a general interest, covering all aspects of new technology from biogenetics to computer systems.

Telephony: Journal of Telecommunications. Telephony Publishing Corp., 55 E. Jackson Blvd., Chicago, ILL 60604. Magazine for telecommunications managers that covers telecommunications issues, developments, and applications.

The Office: Office Publications Inc., 1200 Summer Street, Stamford, CT 06904. Monthly magazine for managers who are looking for information on equipment, automation, and general features. Comprehensive and well presented.

Today's Office: Hearst Business Communications Inc., 645 Stewart Avenue, Garden City, NY 11530. General feature articles with a focus on office automation questions and issues.

Wire Technology: Huebner Publications Inc., 5821 Harper Road, Solon, OH 44139. Stories of interest to manufacturers of wire products. Articles are generally on fiber optics and other wire technology of a technical nature.

Word Processing & Information Systems: Geyer McAllister Publications Inc., 51 Madison Avenue, New York, NY 10010. Practical articles for managers where word processing has been implemented. A general overview of products, issues, etc.

Glossary

A practical and useful list of words utilized by the computer industry, including acronyms and computer jargon.

Access Time: The time required to retrieve information from the computer.

ADAPSO (Association of Data Processing Service Organizations): A trade association for vendors of computer systems, software, and services.

Address: A number specifyng where a unit of information is stored in the computer's memory.

Administrative Support: One of the two broad areas of specialization under word processing, other than typing. Comprises all the nontyping tasks associated with traditional secretarial work.

AI—Artificial Intelligence: Computers doing tasks that, if humans were to do them, would require intelligence.

Algorithm: A complex formula for solving a specific problem.

Alphanumeric Sort: Process in which a word processor puts a list into alphabetical or numerical order, or both.

Analog Transmission: In telecommunications, a means of sending information as a continuous signal of varying magnitudes or frequencies. Distinct from "digital transmission," in which discrete pulses are sent to represent encoded bits of data.

Archive: The procedure of transferring text from on-line system media to off-line storage media.

ASCII (American Standard Code for Information Interchange): A code used in computers and communications systems in which each character, number of special character, is defined in 8 bits (ask-ee).

Assembly Language: Programming language using groups of letters, each group represents a single instruction.

Asynchronous Transmission: A means of sending information whereby each character is individually synchronized by the use of "start" and "stop" bits. Also called start/stop transmission.

Automated Document Storage and Retrieval (ADSTAR): The use of equipment, generally under computer control, to file and recover information in microform.

BASIC (Beginners All Purpose Symbolic Instruction Code): The most widely used computer language, with simple syntax and few commands, often used on microcomputers.

Batch Processing: A collection of similar work that can be processed at one operation in sequential order.

Baud: In telecommunications, a unit of signaling speed, representing the number of discrete conditions or signal events per second. Where each signal event represents two or three bits, 1 baud equals two or three BPs respectively.

BIT: The smallest unit of information that the computer recognizes. A bit is represented by the presence or absence of an electronic pulse, 0 or 1. Effectively, it is one eighth of a byte. For example, a unit which transfers 800 bits per second transfers 100 bytes per second and operates at 1,000 baud.

BISYNC (Binary Synchronmous): An IBM developed communications protocol that has become an industry standard.

Boilerplate Document: One of two initial documents combined to produce a third. It contains that section of the final document which remains constant; for example, the body of a form letter.

Buffer: A storage device that compensates for differences in operating speed or timing between various units of a system.

Byte: A unit of measure in computer storage equal to a sequence of eight adjacent binary digits operated upon as a unit. A byte is to a bit what a word is to a letter. Usually, a bye equals eight bits. To store a mailing list of 100 names in which each name has a maximum of 80 letters, numbers, and spaces, you would need 800 bytes of storage or 8K.

CAD/CAM (Computer Aided Design/Computer Aided Manufacturing): A term applied to efforts to automate design and manufacturing operations.

CAI (Computer Aided Instruction): Using the computer to help teach students. Usually the computer "talks back" to the students, telling them when a mistake is made.

Capturing Keystrokes: The process of recording text as it is typed and stored on some medium, thereby allowing extensive changes to be made without retyping an entire document.

Character: Any coded representation of an alphabet letter, numerical digit, punctuation mark, or symbol.

Chip: A thin silicon wafer on which electronic components are deposited in the form of integrated circuits. Technologically, the key to the microelectronic revolution in computers.

Coaxial Cable: A specially constructed communication line, providing a fairly wide band transmission capabilty, and utilized in many network systems, including cable television.

COBOL (Common Business Oriented Language): A high-level programming language widely used in business applications.

Computer Assisted Retrieval (CAR): The use of a computer to search for and retrieve information relating to the location and description of text or data stored elsewhere on paper or microform.

Computer Input Microfilming (CUM): The rendering of microform images into machine-readable data to permit the information to be revised or manipulated under computer-control.

Computer Output Microfilming (COM): A means of converting digital data from machine to human readable form on microfilm.

CP/M (Control Program for Microprocessors): A popular disk operating system, fast becoming a standard for many of the personal computers and smaller word processing systems, with a vast library of software applications programs available.

CPU (Central Processing Unit): That part of the computer than controls the interpretation and execution of the processing instructions. The "brain" of the computer which performs all the calculations and serves as a switching network for data.

CRT (Cathode Ray Tube): A TV-like screen used by word processors to display work in progress; also known as a video display terminal or VDT.

Cursor: The movable dot on the CRT screen that shows the place on the displayed document for entering new text or making editing changes.

Daisey Wheel: A print element comprising a flat disk with characters around the circumference. Its unique circular design allows these units to print up to 540 words a minute.

DASD (Direct Access Storage Device): A unit of computer equipment that allows direct, quick access to storage for entry or retrieval of information.

Data: The raw information within a computer system.

Data Base: A collection of pieces of data organized, stored, and cross-referenced by the computer. When a large amount of data is involved, such as the complete records of customers or clients, the data base is an important tool for keeping the data organized. It is to data as a filing cabinet is to files.

Data Base Management Systems (DBMS): The software that makes a company's data base integrated; computerized files of information, accessible in multiple ways to many users.

Data Communications: The efficient management of the terminal network functions that make data available to users on a timely and convenient basis.

Data Delivery: The programming required to convert data into useful information for end-users.

Data Processing (DP): The transformation of raw data into useful information by electronic equipment; sometimes referred to as ADP (Automatic Data Processing) or EDP (Electronic Data Processing).

DOS (Disk Operating System): A required program for operating disks. A DOS formats data for storage and retrieval and controls the operation of the disk drive. It usually provides other utilities for naming, renaming, erasing, copying, and transferring data and programs.

Diagnostics: Programs for detecting and isolating a malfunction or mistake in the computer system; features that allow systems or equipment to self-test for flaws.

Direct Connection: The linking of two systems that are compatible by means of wire, cable, or fiber optics. Used primarily for systems that are located close together, because there is a limit to the length of the connection.

Disk: A magnetic storage medium about the size of a 33⅓ RPM record, capable of storing large amounts of data and text, as well as system information. The disk has large storage capacity and an ability to allow the faster random access method of document retrieval. Also known as "hard disk."

Diskette: A magnetic storage medium the size of a 45 RPM record. It is used in word processing applications because it has an ample storage capacity and permits random access document retrieval. Primarily used for text storage, but sometimes stores system information as well. Also known as flexible or floppy disk.

Disk Drive: The peripheral that reads and writes information onto disks. A disk drive is to a disk what a record player is to a record.

Dot Matrix Printer: A high-speed output device that prints characters in a dot matrix pattern.

Downtime: Time when equipment is not in use due to a malfunction.

EDP (Electronic Data Processing): The transformation of raw data into useful information by electronic equipment; sometimes referred to as ADP or automatic data processing.

Electronic Filing: The process by which word processors store information electronically on disks, cards, or tapes.

Electronic Mail: The transmission of inter- and intra-office messages, from one terminal to another, through data communications facilities.

ENIAC (Electronic Numerical Integrator and Calculator): Generally recognized as the first stored-program computer ever built.

External Storage: Any storage medium that can be removed from the system and kept elsewhere; in contrast with "internal storage," which is a physical part of the system.

Facsimile: The transmission of text and illustrative copy electronically, sometimes by radio, but in office operations, more typically by telephone. Facsimile works as follows: Documents scanned on a rotating drum at the sending site are recreated on a comparable drum on the receiving site.

Floppy Disk: The magnetic storage medium primarily used for text storage of word processors. Also referred to as diskette.

Font: The character set a printer is capable of producing. Also, the device that actually produces the character; for example, the IBM "golf ball element," the daisey wheel, the dot matrix array, or print chain element.

Fortran (Formula Translator): A computer language, widely used in scientific and engineering applications.

File Length: Determines the amount of text the word processing file can contain. This is usually measured in "kilobytes" (K), each one equaling 1,024 bytes. Any letter, number, character, or space is a byte.

Global Search and Replace: The process in which a word processor can be used to search through a document for a specific piece of information and then replace it with another.

Graphics: Pictures, charts, drawings, and all other nonalphanumeric displays generated by a computer. Many of the computer systems developed in the 1980s will have graphics capability.

Hard Copy: The printed output of a word processing system, in contrast with "soft copy," which refers to text displayed on the CRT.

Hardware: The physical machinery of the computer processing system as distinct from the "software" or programs, instructions, and training materials.

Information Society: According to reports from the U.S. Bureau of Labor Statistics and Department of Commerce, nearly half the total civilian workforce of the nation work in information related fields such as communications, computers, education, and publishing. Thus, this era of civilization has been dubbed the "information society."

Ink Jet: An imaging method in which characters are electronically "squirt printed" onto a piece of paper.

Intelligent Terminal: A typewriter with a television screen attached to it that can remember things, do calculations, type letters, and communicate with other intelligent terminals.

Interactive: Term applied to word processing typing systems that communicate with computers or other WP terminals, in contrast with "standalone" systems, which are self-contained.

Interface: The point at which two systems, or two devices, or a person and a device interact with one another.

Internal Storage Media: A hard-wired part of a word processing system used to store system information and text. May be either processor memory or disk, and cannot be physically removed from the system.

Justification: Process in which lines of typing begin or end at the same margin, line after line. Typewriters justify typing at the left margin. Many word processors also justify at the right margin.

K: Abbreviation of "kilo," a prefix meaning 1,000; or 1,024. Usually a K is 1024 when referring to memory inside of the computer. An 8K computer therefore has 8,196 bytes of memory. A 70K floppy disk, for example, can store 7,000 bytes.

Keyboard: A device used for entering information into a computer.

Knowledge Worker: Refers to those persons who work in an office, with the responsibility for at least minimal decision making.

Line Printer: An output device characterized by its ability to print one line of text as a single unit.

Magnetic Media: Any of a wide variety of belts, cards, disks, or tapes coated or impregnated with magnetic material for use with the appropriate word processing system, and on which dictation or key strokes are recorded and stored.

Menu: A list of available options displayed on the CRT screen and the system is turned on or after an operation has been completed. Menu-driven systems are those which offer various instructions intermittently as the user needs them to more effectively operate the system.

MIS (Management Information System): A data processing system integrating all the information resources in a company so that one monstrously expensive computer replaces all the smaller units.

Microcomputer: A computer made up of a microprocessor, screen, memory, and interfaces.

Microprocessor: An entire computer "brain" on a slice of silicon about ¼ " square.

Mode: A system function or operating state selected by an operator to achieve a specific result, for example, insert, delete, or merge.

Modem: A device that converts computer data into tones that can be transmitted over ordinary telephone lines and that converts these tones back into data. A modem allows two computers in different locations to exchange data, or for a person with a remote terminal to use a distant computer via a standard telephone.

Network: A number of workstations interconnected by communications channels. These may be cable channels or a central switching device.

OCR (Optical Character Recognition): The machine reading of graphic characters— both letters and numbers—using light-sensitive devices.

OEM (Original Equipment Manufacturer): An organization that purchases computer equipment from the manufacturer and resells it to users after adding value in the form of software or by integrating whole systems.

ON-Line: Any operation taking place under direct control of the CPU.

Operator Prompts: Short, self-explanatory phrases that appear on the CRT during various word processing operations either to guide an operator through an operation or to indicate that an incorrect key has been struck or an illegal procedure has been attempted.

PABX (Private Automatic Branch Exchange): A telephone exchange system that automatically connects interoffice calls and switches incoming calls to in-house extensions.

PASCAL: A popular programming language, similar to BASIC which allows the programmer to structure his ideas more clearly.

Peripheral: A device external to the computer that performs a function, such as storing information, allowing the user to communicate with the computer or transferring information.

Printer: A device that prints information on paper. There are various types of printers that can be attached to computers, depending upon what the user needs for a paper output.

Program: The machine instructions that tell the computer what you want it to do and how to do it. All computers have to be "programmed" before they can perform any useful operations.

Programming Language: The instructions to a computer have to be in one or several languages, such as BASIC, PASCAL, FORTRAN, etc., for the computer to operate. Some computers come with languages already built in (ROM) whereas others must learn a language every time they are turned on.

PROM (Programmable Read Only Memory): A memory that is not programmed during manufacturing and requires a physical or electrical process to program it.

Protocol: A set of rules for the transmission of information.

Proportional Spacing: Means that the space occupied by a character is proportional to the shape of that character. Many of the daisy wheel and dot matrix printers offer proportional spacing as an option, however, not all word processors support this feature.

Queuing Theory: A mathematical procedure useful in predicting how a service with a known capacity will be able to handle various demands made upon it.

RAM (Random Access Memory): A memory in which each element of information has an address (location) and from which any element can be easily and conveniently retrieved by using that address. RAM is the principal memory inside the computer and is used for storing programs and data as they are processed. When the power is turned off, the contents of RAM are lost.

ROM (Read Only Memory): A memory, the data of which cannot be changed by programming. Like PROM, ROM permanently holds programs in the computer's internal memory.

Response Time: The time a system takes to react to a given input.

Scrolling: Process in which a word processor's entire display is moved up and down (vertical scrolling), or right and left (horizontal scrolling).

Shared Logic: Configuration where multiterminal word processing stations are attached to one central processor. This typically uses microprocessor-based intelligent terminals that share disks, tape storage, communications, optical character readers, and other peripherals.

Software: All materials needed to control and operate the "hardware" of an automated system.

State of the Art: The current level of development achieved by an evolving technology.

Standalone Systems: Computer systems that incorporate the screen, keyboard, disk drives, processor, and printer—all within one unit.

Storage Device: A peripheral that stores large amounts of data or programs.

Telecommunications: Communications over a distance via electronic medium, such as cable, satellites, microwave, etc.

Teletypewriter: Generic term for teleprinters and keyboard terminals used in hard-copy communications systems, but distinct from communicating word processors that possess a wide range of text editing capabilities not found in teletypewriters.

Telex: A dial-up teleprinter service of Western Union.

Terminal: A device that has a keyboard, a printer or CRT display, an interface, and sometimes a modem.

Time Sharing: A method that allows two or more users to simultaneously use the same computer. Time sharing essentially divides up the computer's processing time and "shares it" among multiple users.

Tractor Feed: A mechanism that feeds printer paper that has holes punched every half-inch in both margins.

Turnaround Time: The time required for a document to be typed, proofread, corrected, and returned to the word originator. In telecommunications, this refers to the time required to reverse the direction of transmission from send to receive or vice versa.

Unbundling: The pricing separately by word processing equipment suppliers of systems analysis and other support services.

Word Processing: Computing dedicated to the particular application of placing characters on the page and manipulating those characters as often as necessary before a final printout is prepared.

Word Wraparound: A feature of some word processors that allows them to automatically close up any resulting gaps that may occur when text is edited.

Checklist and Guidelines for the Office Manager and Executive

CHECKLIST NO. 1

Daily Task Analysis

Many activities carried out on a daily basis need to be analyzed in terms of the number of hours spent on specific chores by both secretaries and managers. For each of the following activities estimate the percent of time spent.

		Percent
1.	Handwritten Work	
	Letters	_____
	Memos	_____
	Forms	_____
	Reports	_____
	Procedures	_____
	Posting (lists, logs, worksheets)	_____
	Calendar maintenance (number of entries)	_____
	Other _____	_____

2. Mail Handling
   Interdepartment mail   _____

   To and from noncompany locations   _____

   Use of wire service (telex)   _____

   Mass Mailings   _____

3. Telephone Use
   General business discussion   _____

   Follow up on activities   _____

   Scheduling/confirming meetings   _____

4. Typing
   Creating original documents   _____

   Editing/revising documents   _____

   Proofing documents   _____

   Other _____   _____

5. Copying
   Carbon copies   _____

   Copier   _____

   Reproduction services   _____

   (What percent need collation?)   _____

6. Meetings
   Informal (nonscheduled meetings)   _____

   Formal meetings   _____

7. Searching/Retrieving/Assembling information
   Searching through files   _____

   Research using telephone   _____

   Library search   _____

   Filing data back into files   _____

8. Calculating
   Original calculations done manually   _____

   Using a calculator/adding machine   _____

   Using a data processor   _____

   Recalculating/verifying/proofing   _____

9. Reading/Reviewing materials
   Reading material prepared by others   _____

   Reading material prepared by you (proofing)   _____

   General professional reading   _____

   Other _____   _____

10. Original creative work
    Written work   _____

    Data analysis   _____

    Visual graphics   _____

CHECKLIST NO. 2

Records/File Management

Records management and filing is a large part of office processing and takes a great deal of time. The following questions look at filing duties in the office...

1. How often do you usually file?

   _____ daily

   _____ weekly

   _____ monthly

   _____ other (specify)

2. How are documents filed?

   _____ by name

   _____ by number

   _____ by topic

   _____ other (specify)

3. Location of the files

   _____ percent at your workplace

   _____ percent at a remote location

4. Is your present file space adequate?

   _____ yes

   _____ no

6. Of the files you are currently using what percent are

   _____ active, relate directly to your work

   _____ inactive—for storage only

   _____ confidential

   _____ duplicated elsewhere

7. Indicate the number of multiple copies of a document filed for cross-reference purposes.

   _____ one   _____ three

   _____ two   _____ four

   _____ five or more

8. Are all of the principals of the company or department familiar with the filing procedure?

   _____ yes   _____ no

9. Is there any special protection for vital records (confidential material)

   _____ yes   _____ no

   _____ not applicable

10. If a person were assigned to find a file on a specific piece of information which dates back six months how long would that take to complete?

_____ under an hour

_____ an hour

_____ over an hour

CHECKLIST NO. 3

Keyboarding Activities

Time spent at a keyboard is a large factor in most offices, especially by the secretaries, but in some businesses by managers too. This checklist will indicate how current keyboarding activities are currently handled and by whom and will indicate where some of the deficiencies may be.

1. What kind of keyboarding device do you use?

_____ Manual typewriter

_____ Electric typewriter

_____ Electronic typewriter

_____ Mag card or memory typewriter

_____ Video display

_____ None

_____ Other (specify)

2. What percent of your typing originates from (total should equal 100%)

_____% machine dictation

_____% shorthand

_____% longhand

_____% typed copy

_____% self composed

_____% other (specify)

3. On the average, how many hours does it take for document completion from the time of the document to the typing of the finished document?

_____ One hour

_____ One day

_____ One week

_____ Longer

4. Before a final copy is produced, how often is it retyped? (percentage of times)

_____% one time   _____% three times

_____% two times   _____% four times or more

5. What percent of your work is confidential in nature and cannot be sent to a typing pool or someone else?

_____ 80–100%   _____ 20–40%

_____ 60–80%   _____ 0–20%

_____ 40–60%   _____ Does not apply

6. How much time do you estimate that you would save if you never had to rekeyboard a document?

_____ 80–100%   _____ 20–40%

_____ 60–80%   _____ 0–20%

_____ 40–60%   _____ Does not apply

CHECKLIST NO. 4

Electronic Information Processing

A great deal of information that is currently manually processed could be processed using automation. The following questionnaire looks at the analysis of what electronic systems might fit into your office environment to automate certain tasks that now are handled manually.

1. Word Processing Systems:
   A. Do word processing systems fit into your office scheme?

   _____ yes

   _____ no

   B. How many word processing terminals do you feel that you need to replace existing typewriter workstations?

   _____ one

   _____ more than three

   _____ several

   (The number here indicates whether you need to look at standalones or a multi-terminal configuration.)

   C. Do you produce finished typeset documents?

   _____ occasionally

   _____ frequently

   _____ constantly

   (The answer to this question gives you the information to consider whether or not you need a direct interface between word processing and phototypesetting.)

   D. Would you use word processing terminals for: (check all that apply)

   _____ Typing functions

   _____ Editing

   _____ Information retrieval

_____ Database access

_____ Data input

_____ Math functions

_____ Sort and search tasks, such as list processing

_____ Calendar and tickler file

_____ Electronic mail boxes

_____ All of the above

_____ Other (specify) _____

2. Optical Character Readers

A. Do you have large volumes of paper processed daily?

_____ yes   _____ no

B. Is most of this paperwork done currently on an electric or electronic typewriter?

_____ yes   _____ no

C. Do you have cabinets filled with back files that would need to be input on a word processor?

_____ yes   _____ no

D. Is the office budget able to afford an OCR which sells for upwards of $20,000?

_____ yes   _____ no

(The answers to these questions will give you an indication of whether or not an OCR should be considered.)

3. Data Processing Systems

A. How is data now handled by the office?

1. _____ by a bookkeeper using manual procedures.

2. _____ with a calculator/adding machine.

3. _____ by an outside service that handles all of the office's accounting procedures.

B. Is the payroll done inhouse or outside?

_____ inhouse

_____ outside

If answer is outside, what is the cost $ _____ per week

C. How are budgets prepared?

1. _____ through a central group within the company.

2. _____ individually by each department manager.

3. _____ combination of above.

D. What is the volume of accounts receivables and payables each week?

1. _____ number of pieces of paper per week generated for amount of paper-handling for accounts receivables.

2. _____ number of pieces of paper generated for accounts payables.

E. How many persons are involved in doing all accounting and billing tasks necessary to the business?

1. _____ more than 10
2. _____ 6–10 persons
3. _____ 4–6 persons
4. _____ 2–4 persons
5. _____ one person
6. _____ Does not apply

4. Business Graphics
   A. How frequently do you have the need to incorporate visual illustrations or graphics in your documents?

   _____ often

   _____ sometimes

   _____ rarely

   _____ does not apply

   B. Does your company employ a staff to handle graphics?

   _____ yes   _____ no

   C. If the answer is yes, how many individuals are employed in this task?

   _____ 1–3

   _____ 4–6

   _____ 6–10

   _____ more than 10

   D. Do you feel that you need a graphics terminal?

   _____ yes   _____ no

   E. Do you feel you need a terminal that has graphics capability with the appropriate software?

   _____ yes   _____ no

5. Decision Support System
   A. Are the executives in your company willing to utilize a terminal?

   _____ yes   _____ no

   B. If you had an executive workstation what would you use it for? (check all that apply)

   _____ inventory management

   _____ forecasting

   _____ budget preparation

   _____ calendar

   _____ tickler file

   _____ electronic mailbox

   _____ general word processing

_____ graphics

_____ database access

_____ other (specify) _____

C. What features would you like on an executive workstation? (check all that apply)

_____ text editing

_____ information retrieval

_____ sort

_____ global search and replace

_____ math capabilities

_____ graphics

_____ ability to handle electronic mail

_____ spelling verification

_____ programmability (in English)

_____ ease of use (training of no more than two hours)

_____ voice input rather than keyboard

_____ communications

_____ other (specify) _____

5. Electronic Mail

A. Is your company large enough to support an internal electronic mail system?

_____ yes   _____ no

C. Estimate the time you spend on mail activities each day (minutes/hours):

_____ opening mail

_____ reading mail

_____ answering mail

D. Estimate the time you spend each day on activities which electronic mail might handle for you:

_____ scheduling meetings

_____ telephone "tag"

_____ writing memos

_____ other (specify) _____

CHECKLIST NO. 5
System Architecture

The individual features of a system are important to the ultimate success with which the system will fit into your office environment. The following checklist attempts to provide most of the considerations you need in selecting a system.

1. General hardware configuration
   _____ Nondisplay editing system
   _____ Electronic typewriter
   _____ Memory typewriter
   _____ Removable media typewriter (Mag card system)
   _____ Display systems
   _____ Standalone word processors
   _____ Shared resource word processing
   _____ Shared logic word processing
   _____ Small business computers
2. Screen Size
   _____ Partial page display
   _____ Full page display
   _____ Thin window display
3. Disk Drives
   _____ Single disk drive
   _____ Dual disk drive
   _____ Hard disk
4. Printer Characteristics
   _____ Letter quality
   _____ High speed
   _____ Noise
   _____ Automatic feeder
5. Word Processing System Characteristics
   _____ Easy to use
   _____ Tiltable screen
   _____ Detachable keyboard
   _____ Contrast and brightness controls
   _____ Stability of display (does it flicker or blur?)
   _____ Legibility of characters (clarity)
   _____ Layout of keys on keyboard (easy to understand)
   _____ Cursor positioning
   _____ Prompts available
   _____ Menus for training
   _____ Help button
   _____ Display—size, color, zoom or magnify

_____ Ease of use of search function

_____ Horizontal and vertical scrolling

_____ Placement of footnotes, tables

_____ Pagination capability

_____ Characteristics of delete command

_____ Formatting

_____ Headers and footers

_____ Underlining and boldface

_____ Availability of "windows"

_____ Ease in moving blocks of text around

CHECKLIST NO. 6
Selecting a Vendor

The choice of vendor is critical to the success of your transition to office automation. Some vendor companies have more experience and knowledge than others in particular use markets. Some are financially stable, others are not. Some have a reputation for supporting their systems and for their reliability in meeting service commitments. Some of the issues to consider when selecting the vendor include the following:

1. Is the vendor a

   _____ manufacturer

   _____ distributor

   _____ a third party

2. How long has the vendor been in the computer business?

   _____ more than 20 years

   _____ 11–20 years

   _____ 5–10 years

   _____ 2–5 years

   _____ less than 2 years

3. Is the vendor company a subsidiary of a larger corporate entity?

   _____ yes   _____ no

4. Does the vendor sell to markets throughout the world?

   _____ yes   _____ no

5. Over the past few years has the vendor's sales record

   _____ increased

   _____ remained stable

   _____ declined

6. How large is the vendor's overall user base?

_____ over 50,000

_____ 20,001–50,000

_____ 5,001–20,000

_____ 1,000–5,000

_____ less than 1,000

7. How large is the user base of the particular system you are planning to purchase?

_____ over 50,000

_____ 20,001–50,000

_____ 5,001–20,000

_____ 1,000–5,000

_____ less than 1,000

8. How many service locations does the vendor have in the United States?

_____ over 150

_____ 76–150

_____ 26–75

_____ 10–25

_____ less than 10

9. What is the turnaround time that the vendor promises on a repair call?

_____ 4–6 hours

_____ 2–4 hours

_____ more than the above

_____ less than the above

10. Does the vendor also provide a full line of peripheral products (printers, telecommunications, etc.)?

_____ yes   _____ no

11. Will the vendor provide: (check all that apply)

_____ hardware

_____ software

_____ installation

_____ training

_____ support

_____ service

_____ documentation

12. Will the vendor quote all costs separately?

_____ yes   _____ no

13. Does the vendor accept full responsibility for the following:

	All	Some	None
Pre-Sale system analysis	___	___	___
Equipment delivery	___	___	___
System design	___	___	___
Software support	___	___	___
Installation	___	___	___
Training	___	___	___
Continuing aid	___	___	___

14. Will the vendor's own staff support and maintain the operating systems?

_____ yes   _____ no

15. If there is a future problem will the vendor correct it at no cost?

_____ yes   _____ no

16. Does the vendor provide a written proposal prior to purchase with everything written out clearly?

_____ yes   _____ no

17. Is the vendor proposing custom or packaged software?

_____ custom   _____ standard

18. If custom software is required, will the vendor provide you with a written outline of what is needed and how to get it?

_____ yes   _____ no

19. Will the vendor demonstrate the equipment using an action application similar to one you will need?

_____ yes   _____ no

20. Are the training manual and all other documentation clearly understandable?

_____ yes   _____ no

21. If it is necessary for the vendor to initiate an engineering change for a system component, will your system be modified free of charge?

_____ always   _____ sometimes   _____ never

22. Who will provide the maintenance for the system?

_____ vendor   _____ third party

23. If the maintenance is not supplied by vendor, does the maintenance group service vendor's products exclusively?

_____ yes   _____ no

24. How often is routine maintenance performed in the vendor's standard maintenance contract?

_____ monthly

_____ quarterly

_____ three times a year

_____ semiannually

_____ never

25. Are add-on components such as a new printer, disk drives, etc., sold and serviced by the same vendor?

_____ yes   _____ no

Index